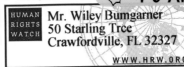
# KNOWING GOD

# THROUGH

# PRAYER

## Wiley Bumgarner

Publisher: Ralph Roberts

Editor: Pat Roberts

Cover Design: ©2001 Ralph Roberts
Interior Design & Electronic Page Assembly: **WorldComm®**

The text of this book is not copyrighted and may be freely copied and distributed.

10  9  8  7  6  5  4  3  2

ISBN  1-57090-156-2

**Mountain Church**—a division of Creativity, Inc.—is a full–service publisher located at 65 Macedonia Road, Alexander NC 28701. Phone (828) 252–9515, Fax (828) 255–8719. For orders only: 1-800-472-0438. Visa and MasterCard accepted.

**Mountain Church** is distributed to the trade by Midpoint Trade Books, Inc., 27 West 20th Street, New York NY 10011, (212) 727-0190, (212) 727-0195 fax.

This book is also available on the internet in the **Publishers CyberMall.** Set your browser to http://www.abooks.com and enjoy the many fine values available there.

# Foreword

During the year 2000, I wrote an average of a prayer each day. I wrote these prayers during periods of Bible study and meditiation. These prayers express my sincere desires and are usually inspired by some verse of Scripture. I beleieve that anyone who will read these prayers will come to know God better. I have tried to write words of truth and inspiration. One may read them one at a time as a daily devotion, or one may read several at one sitting.

I believe that to know God is to experience the best in life. I hope these prayers will enable you to experience truth and to avoid falsehood. I believe that the good life is achieved by learning truth. God is truth. Satan is false. Evangelism and missions are helping us to move from Satan unto God. To know God is to live. Jesus came to reveal God to us that we might live abundantly. If we accept Jesus as the revelation of God, we will pray without ceasing. As we pray without ceasing, we continually seek to live more abundantly.

As you read and meditate on these prayers, may you communicate with God and share peace, joy, love, and understanding. May your life be enriched as you share peace, joy, and love with others. May Jesus Christ be your Lord and Saviour. May you live, move, and have your being in God. May you be guided by the Holy Spirit of truth and love.

I would like to thank all the authors whose books and articles I have read with special thanks to Oswald Chambers for the **My Utmost for His Highest Journal,** where I recorded my prayers for the year.

# About The Author

Wiley C. Bumgarner is a native of Haywood County, North Carolina. He was born in Waynesville, North Carolina on March 22, 1919.

Wiley is the son of the late Julius Pinkney Bumgarner and Julia Lanning Bumgarner. Wiley had seven brothers, all older than he and two sisters. One sister, who is still living, is younger than he is. His brothers and older sister are all deceased.

Wiley grew up on a small farm during the Great Depression. He worked several years as a construction worker before serving in the U.S. Navy throughout World War II.

After the war, Wiley attended Mars Hill College, Furman University, Southern Baptist Theological Seminary, and Arizona State University.

Wiley has pastored Baptist churches, has taught history and English, and has served as a realtor.

Wiley lives with his wife, Hazel, to whom he has been married since February 17, 1946. They reside in Asheville, North Carolina.

Wiley and Hazel have one son, Barry, and three grandchildren.

# Being Right With God

Having confessed one's sins and turned away from them.

Having become a follower of the Lord and being receptive to the guidance of the Holy Spirit.

Having accepted the revelation of God in Christ.

Having turned to God in faith and reverence.

Having turned from worshipping self to worshipping God. As Paul would say, "Having crucified the old man and turned to a living God."

Having humbled oneself and accepted God as the Sovereign ruler of one's life.

Having through prayer and meditation overcome deceit, conceit, arrogance, and bigotry.

Having turned away from seeking worldly, degenerating, and dissipating pleasures to seeking joy in serving one's fellow beings.

Having turned away from lusting after power, money, and sex to seeking first the rule of God.

Having developed concern and compassion for those less fortunate than oneself.

Having developed curiosity and interest in the welfare of all people.

Having developed a sincere love for truth.

Having learned that following Jesus is a way of life, not a religious superstition.

Having learned that love for others is the basic principle of righteous living.

Having developed moral standards based on the teaching of Jesus and his followers.

Having rejected false teaching and hypocrisy.

Having learned that all truth is of God, and all falsehood or deception is against God.

Having learned that all wisdom is of God.

Having learned that redemption concerns all of life.

Having learned that God is ever present.

Having learned that one may deceive one's self but not God.

Having learned that one reaps what one sows and cannot do wrong without suffering the consequences.

Having learned that God has no favorites. His laws apply equally to all people everywhere.

Having learned that truth doesn't have to be defended. It stands on its merits.

Having learned that voting doesn't solve problems. Voting only shows which side one is on. Problems are solved by people reaching an understanding and coming to a consensus.

Having learned that Scriptures should be understood before being quoted. One should quote meanings, if one is to be helpful.

Having learned that prayer is sincere desire and must be positive to get good results.

Having learned the difference between piosity and piousness. Piosity is acting or pretense. Piousness is living truth.

Having learned that one cannot change God's laws and that God never works contrary to law. God's laws govern the universe. To disobey or ignore God's laws is to indulge in futility and/or destruction.

Having learned that true principles are permanent. Only methods change.

Having learned that no one is in a position to flatter God. The universe can exist with us or without us.

Having learned that our knowledge of God is never complete. One should continue to learn.

Having learned that God is a friend to all who will do his will. We are our own enemies when we work against God.

Having learned that God owns the universe. Human beings are God's stewards. It is required of stewards that they be faithful. The steward that is unfaithful receives curses instead of blessings.

Having learned that too many possessions become a curse. To most of us, it is more blessed to give than to receive. Whether we give or receive we should be gracious.

Having learned that God's laws apply to all of life. With God there is no sacred and secular.

Having learned that with God there is no time and eternity. God's eternity is now.

Having learned that God is not changed by human emotions. God is reality. God is truth. God is love.

Having learned that the universe is without limit as to time or space. Therefore knowledge cannot ever be complete.

Having learned that today is the day for salvation. One cannot skip time. One can't live day after tomorrow until they pass through tomorrow. We live one day at a time.

Having learned that the good life is not possessions, but knowledge, wisdom, and understanding that enable us to live discretely and to show good will.

Having learned that peace comes with unity and unity comes with understanding and good will.

Having learned that Divine love is God's active good will toward all his creation.

Having learned that love of God and love of humanity are the same. One can't love God and hate his creation.

Having learned that inner peace and joy are always possible for God-fearing people.

Having learned that God is worthy of our devotion, our honor, and our praise. We glorify God by making him known. When we make God known, we promote life. In God is life. Apart from God is death.

Having become right with God, we will bear witness to the saving grace manifested through Jesus Christ. Our prayer or sincere desire is that others may come to know God, for we believe that to know God through personal faith is to become a partaker of eternal life.

Having become a partaker of eternal life, one will show it by loving others. It is by expressing love in deed and truth that one brings glory to God. Our mission in this age is to glorify God.

# Love

Love is the identifying mark of the follower of Christ. One may have many virtues, but without love he will have little influence for good.

Love is an active expression of good will. It is a unifying force. It makes friends of enemies and lovers of friends

Love is a redemptive power. It makes evil good, good better, and better best. It carries the possessor into higher and higher places until finally he or she is at home with God.

Love grows as it is shared. The more we give away the more we have. Love verifies the saying, "The liberal soul shall be made fat."

Love adds grace to other virtues. It makes life rich. Love is a catalyst that makes other virtues work faster and bear more fruit.

Love makes temperance meaningful. It helps us to give and take with grace. It is a rebuke to evil and the praise of the good.

Love makes silence golden. It helps us to enjoy being alone and to enjoy listening while others speak.

Love makes order out of chaos. It brings minds together instead of tearing them apart.

Love resolves problems. It goes to the heart of things. Instead of covering up, suppressing, or evading, it removes the barriers and makes solutions possible.

Love promotes thrift. It gives value to time and effort. It enables us to accomplish more with less effort.

Love makes one more industrious. It makes work a joy and service a pleasure. It makes experiencing life a reward in itself.

Love promotes justice. One who loves others is never unfair. Justice tempered with mercy is a habit as well as a rule.

Love promotes moderation. Love is always considerate. It helps to avoid extremes which are offensive to others.

Love promotes cleanliness. One who loves others desires a clean environment, clean hands, and a pure heart.

Love promotes peace. One who loves others tries to be congenial. He wants to attract, rather than repel.

Love promotes chastity. It leads to purity and wholeness. One who loves never forces himself on others.

Love makes one humble. The one who loves, exalts others rather than himself. Helping others is the mark of love.

Love is expressing and sharing the fellowship of God. It is the mark of one who belongs to the family of God.

Love has been described as the master wheel. It is what makes everything else work. It undergirds other virtues.

Love is the preservative that keeps life from spoiling. It repels the small enemies—"the little foxes that spoil the grapes."

Love is an ingredient that adds flavor to life. Love makes life more zestful.

Love when added to tongue or pen keeps us from regretfully saying, "It might have been."

Love can't be bought or sold. It is more precious than silver or gold.

Love will keep you from trouble and strife if you apply it daily to all of your life.

Love will help you on life's road. It will ease your burden and lighten your load.

Love will help you the victory to win in your personal battle with the demon sin.

Love is the music of the angelic band announcing the good will of God and man.

Love enriches life, every part. Meet each day with love in your heart. Hear the words of Jesus that ring anew, "Love one another as I love you."

Love is the active expression of good will resulting in good deeds.

Love is the attitude of gratitude toward God and one's fellow beings.

Love is the release of good emotions.

Love is the seeking of wholesome fellowship.

Love is the promotion of peaceful relationships.

Love is the mutual helpfulness of people who respect each other.

Love is the sharing of one's self and one's possessions with others.

Love is giving to the person in need.

Love is visiting the sick, the shut-in, the bereaved, or the imprisoned.

Love is helping to feed the hungry, heal the sick, or clothe the naked.

Love is giving hope to the discouraged.

Love is giving rest to the tired and weary, or giving work to the idle.

Love is educating and inspiring the young.

Love is helping to carry the burdens of the middle-aged.

Love is comforting, respecting, and caring for the aged.

Love is the making and enforcing of good laws.

Love is removing hindrances to progress.

Love is preserving and developing resources for good.

Love is upholding truth, honesty, and justice.

Love is having a spirit of peace, kindness, tolerance, and under-standing.

Love is a gift of God and an expression of the character of God.

Love is the spirit of Christ at work in the lives of individuals.

Love is the work of God's Holy Spirit creating the New Heaven and the New Earth.

Love is Christians witnessing to a lost world to the saving grace of Jesus Christ.

Love is parents giving themselves sacrificially for their children.

Love is children honoring, respecting, and cooperating with their parents.

Love is employees doing honest and efficient labor for their employers.

Love is employers providing good wages and good working conditions for employees.

Love is different nations of people working together for harmony and peace.

Love is the essence of the abundant life.

Love is the glue that holds all human relationships together.

Love is the greatest of virtues, for Love is God and God is Love.

# January

Dear God,

I am grateful for a new year. I look forward to sharing the good news of you, my God. I am full of hope for good things to come. I seek your truth and love.

Give me knowledge, understanding, and wisdom that I may serve you faithfully. Accept my gratitude, and forgive my sins. Help me to see your goodness and to make it known to others. May I be inspired to live an honest, truthful, and useful life. Help me to be for others what I would like for others to be for me. Help me to make this day, this week, this year, this decade, this century better by my having been here. In Jesus Name, Amen!

Dear God,

Give us faith to go where we have not been and to do what we have not done. Help us to learn what we do not know and to see what we have not seen. Help us to be more alert and to be more aware of others. Help us to see from the other person's view. Help us to make the goodness about us known. May we see no evil, hear no evil, and do no evil. Give us open minds that we may acquire knowledge, understanding, and wisdom.

Be with us each day as we journey through life. Help us to use our time and means wisely. Give us more faith. Amen!

Dear God,

May each of us accept our responsibilities. May we enjoy our freedom. May we accept others. May we be sincere and helpful. Enrich our experiences. Help us to learn. Give us more wisdom.

We know there are dark clouds around us. Help us to see through the clouds. Help us to see the rainbow and be reminded of all that is good. Lighten our path. Help us to see our way. May we be mindful of the goodness of others. Help us to show gratitude. Forgive our sins and help us to forgive others. Be merciful to us and help us to be merciful. Guide us we pray. Amen!

January 4

Dear God,

We thank you for your Son Jesus; may we follow him today. Help us to accept Jesus as Lord. Help us to be committed to his example. May we see you as Jesus reveals you. May we be wise and not foolish. May we seek to know truth and to do good. May we have good fellowship and understanding. May we learn and do your will. Give us patience and courage. Help us to face reality. May our thoughts and actions help us to be healthy, wealthy, and wise.

Amen.

January 5

Dear God,

Give us more knowledge, understanding, and wisdom. May we learn to follow Jesus as we grow in grace. Give us more faith. May we face reality. May we overcome temptation and do what is relevant. Help us to be good stewards. May we use our time, talents, and other resources wisely. Help us to forgive and be forgiven. Help us to be useful. May we help others to live more abundantly. Give us peace that we may prosper. Help us to be peacemakers that we may be called your children. Thank you.

Amen!

January 6

Dear God,

May our dwelling place be with you. May we so live as to make your presence welcome. May we not be ashamed, but be righteous, and stand for our convictions with lion-like boldness. Help us to mature. May we overcome our childish ways. May we come to say with Jesus, "Not as I will, but as you will." Deliver us from anyone who would lead us to do evil. May we overcome evil with good. Help us to experience your goodness and to share it with others. May we be stewards of good as well as being good stewards.

Amen!

January 7

Dear God,

May we come to know Jesus through experience. May Jesus be not only with us, but also in us. May the Spirit of Jesus lead us to love as he loves. May we go about doing good. May we relate to others as one people with one Spirit and one God. May all we say and do be in harmony with truth. May we do good, seek to be righteous, and speak what is true. Help us to separate what is confused. Enlighten us until we can see your purpose. Help us to move forward and upward.

Amen!

January 8

Dear God,

May we be willing to sacrifice ourselves for your glory. May we obey your laws. We know that obedience is better than sacrifice. Give us the wisdom and the willingness to do what is good, right, and true. May we choose to face reality with gratitude. We confess our sins and seek more faith. May we continue to learn and to use our knowledge. May we have mutual blessings and be a true fellowship. May we overcome evil with good. May we promote peace and harmony. May we have the Holy Spirit of Truth and love that we may follow Jesus in revealing you to the age.

Amen!

January 9

Dear God,

Help me today to do what is good, right, true, and beautiful. Help me to be wise. Help me to do what is relevant. Help me to do what needs to be done when it needs to be done. Forgive me my debts and help me to be grateful. May I see from the other person's point of view. May I do unto others what I would like for others to do unto me. May I grow in grace and increase in knowledge, understanding, wisdom, May my thoughts, meditations, and spoken words be relevant. Guide me by your Holy Spirit.

Amen!

January 10

Dear God,

I pray today that I may be humble enough to accept your blessings. Give to me such blessings as I may give to others. May I be willing, able, and ready to share as I have opportunity. May I help others to live more abundantly. Accept my gratitude and forgive my sins. Increase my faith. May I grow in grace, increase in knowledge, understand better, and live joyously. May our fellowship grow healthier, wealthier, and wiser. Guide us we pray.

Amen!

January 11

Dear God,

What can I do today to make you known as you are? Help me to face reality. Help me to do good, live right, and learn truth. Give me insight, vision, and determination. Help me to be an example of one who believes in Jesus. Help me to help others as well as myself. Give me the Spirit of Jesus. Help me to create a peaceful environment where all of us working together can learn to live more abundantly. May we each accept responsibility.

Amen!

January 12

Dear God,

In the quietness of the hour, I pray for more knowledge of you. Reveal your wisdom, love, and truth to me. Help me to have union with you. Show me the way to go. Help me to know truth and to experience true freedom. May I no longer feel the bonds of sin. May I overcome ignorance, superstition, all false-hood, and ill will. Forgive my sins, and help me to be grateful. Guide my thoughts and my actions. Thank you for this day. May the words of my mouth and my deepest thoughts be acceptable.

Amen!

January 13

Dear God,

We realize that we must speak to you alone. We ask in faith. We believe in your laws. Give us more knowledge, more understanding, and more wisdom. May we be as the Inner Circle who asked of Jesus, "Give us according to our faith." We trust your wisdom. Help us to be faithful that we may share our wisdom. May we learn and teach. Help us to be willing to learn before we try to teach. May we be slow to speak but swift to hear. Help us to be effective teachers. Help us to live so as to inspire others. Forgive our sins and guide us.

Amen!

January 14

Dear God,

We are in your hands. Send us where you will. Use us as your servants. May we do what is good, right, and sincere. Hear our prayers. Forgive our sins. Give us strength. May we be fruitful. Help us to so live as to make your goodness and mercy known. May we work without shirking our duty. May we be of mutual benefit to all whom we serve. Help us to help others. May we love one another and do unto others, as we would have them do unto us. May we have malice toward none.

Amen!

January 15

Dear God,

May we be sincerely baptized. May we have died to sin and been resurrected to walk in a newness of life. May we be a true fellowship that is worthy of being called a church. May we share all our blessings. May we be good stewards of all our possessions. May we be sincere ministers. May we meet human need. May we be good examples of all we teach or proclaim. May we accept responsibility and refrain from blaming others. May each of us become healthy, wealthy, and wise. Help us to live more abundantly.

Amen!

January 16

Dear God,

Help us to hear clearly. May we hear your voice and heed your call. May we understand your word and do your will. May we so live as to reflect your light. May we have open minds and think often. May we prove all things and hold fast to what is good. Help us to think before we speak. Help us to listen to others when they speak. Help us to examine before we evaluate. Help us to accept the changes of life and our environment. May we work toward making life better. When we have done our duty, may we be content.

Amen!

January 17

Dear God,

May we live as true children of yours. May your love be seen in us. May we reveal you to all whom we influence. May we help to bring about your kingdom and be loyal to that kingdom. May your will be our will. Turn us from evil. Forgive our debts. Make us grateful. May we see the beauty of nature and the goodness of people. May we remember to sow good seed, so that we may reap good fruit. May all we think, say, and do be helpful. May we learn to know when things are relevant. May we make wise choices.

Amen!

January 18

Dear God,

Help me to live an honest, consistent, and persevering life. May I be honest, truthful, and consistent. Help me to think or listen before I speak and while I am talking. May I be truthful and relevant. Help me to speak loud enough to be heard by each person to whom I am speaking. May I never raise my voice or speak vile words that show anger or wrath unless it is relevant to do so. May I rebuke with softness and sincerity. May I readily confess and repent when in error. Give me the grace to tolerate what I cannot change. Give me the courage to pursue change that is needed and relevant. Give me wisdom and discretion.

Amen!

January 19

Dear God,

Help me to hear your voice and to heed your message. Help me to discern truth and trends. May I never pretend to know truth when I am only half informed. May I always be ready to say, "I don't know," if that is the relevant answer. May I be a play actor only when people know I am acting. May I not dramatize what is foolish. Help me to have a good sense of humor—one that shows good sense. May I always add to wisdom rather than foolishness. May I be an example of a prophet rather than a judge.
Amen!


January 20

Dear God,

Thank you for bringing me into this world and allowing me to live. Thank you for allowing me to choose to live like Jesus. Forgive my weakness and shortcomings. Thank you for your Spirit of truth and love. May I live according to your will and not be manipulated by those of ignorance or ill will. Help me to desire to do right and to learn what is right. Forgive my prejudices—known and unknown. Help me to love others and to show it by doing what is right and relevant.
Amen!


January 21

Dear God,

Help me to know you and to know myself. May I understand and respect our relationship. May I be who I am, and recognize you for who you are. May I see others as they are. Thank you for the right to be free. May I never abuse that right. May I be humble enough to learn and intelligent enough to understand. May I be blessed and be a blessing. May I have faith to act and the will to act when it is relevant. Give me patience to wait and renewed strength. Thank you for both work and rest. Help me to enjoy life. Forgive my sins.
Amen!

January 22

Dear God,

Go with me today. May I feel your presence. Help me to relate to others and to enjoy the relationship. Help me to be an example rather than a judge. Help me to do right and to forgive sin. May I reflect light. Help me to be helpful and not harmful. Help me to grow in grace and gratitude. Help me to see and enjoy the good, the right, the true, and the beautiful. Help me to see, encourage, and enrich the good in others. Help me to live a wholesome life today and be prepared for a better tomorrow. Thank you for all the prosperity in the world.

Amen!

January 23

Dear God,

I thank you just now for all your goodness that is being manifested throughout the earth. Thank you for all the peace and prosperity. Thank you for all the health, wealth, and wisdom. Thank you for all the many development that enhance the joy of living. Thank you for all the opportunities that our generation enjoys. Thank you for the wonders of today and the hope of a better tomorrow. Thank you for all the great scientists, and technicians. Thank you for the many people who are helping to conquer disease and to avoid war, strife, and accidents. Thank you for helping us to enjoy life.

Amen!

January 24

Dear God,

You have shown me that to love and serve you is to show good will and do good for the mutual benefit of all. You have shown me that, "Life is real. Life is earnest." Life to me is not a ritual, a pretense, a pious act, or ceremony. Thank you for your truth. Help me to so live that my life will make a difference in the lives of others. May I be a good example. May I not only try to be moral, but also relate properly to others, and be careful to also face reality. May I be mindful of others. May I be willing to die for others as Jesus did.

Amen!

January 25

Dear God,

Help me to acquire knowledge, understanding, and wisdom. Help me to be humble enough to learn truth until I have become able to rightly divide truth. May I always remember the difference between ritual and reality. May I remember to do righteous acts rather than to act righteous. Thank you for your consistence in being faithful in obeying your laws, which you have wisdom to obey. May I acquire wisdom and be discrete so that I, too, may obey your laws. Thank you for allowing me to know Jesus of Nazareth. He is my example and my teacher. Help me to be sincere and wise as Jesus is. Forgive my sins.

Amen!

January 26

Dear God,

I thank you for making us of more value than the things used for fuel and/or food. Thank you for helping us to have mental and/or spiritual assets. May we become wise enough to know you as Lord of the harvest as well as Creator of the seed. May we live by faith as we await the time of harvest. Forgive us when we seek miracles or short cuts. Help us to have true faith. May we not be as those wicked people who need signs and wonders. May we seek reality and experience it by faith.

Amen!

January 27

Dear God,

Help us to live for the mutual benefit of all that we be not selfish. May we know that you are one God and we are one people. Help us to do as Jesus does and teaches. May we "Love others as ourselves, and do unto others as we would have them do unto us." Thank you for giving us Jesus to reveal you and your will. Help us to know Jesus better that we may know you better. May we have such faith that in doing good, serving others, and seeking truth we can forget our troubles.

Amen!

January 28

Dear God,

May we come to know that you are with your people, and that we deal with you as we deal with people. May we repent by changing our attitude and our deeds. Take away the beams from our eyes and help us to see ourselves as we are and to see others as you see them. May we not be judgmental but show mercy and have compassion. May we see others as friends and not enemies. May we come to know that those whom we label as enemies can be our salvation. Give us more tolerance. Give us more faith. Help us to be good examples.

Amen!

January 29

Dear God,

Reveal yourself to us that we may know you better. Help us to become more and more receptive to your revelation. May others see your invisible Spirit in us. May our thoughts, our words, and our deeds reveal your love. Help us to love others as we love ourselves and to do unto them, as we would have you do unto us. May we all come to accept your eternal, unchanging law of reciprocity. May we all have mutual love. May all that we do be helpful in some way to all concerned. Give us more wisdom and more faith.

Amen!

January 30

Dear God,

May we all become more reluctant to spread bad news. May we respect our elders and our superiors. May we obey your laws and appreciate those who teach us. May we seek clarification of what we do not understand. May we be awakened to our surroundings. May we have insight and foresight. Help us to become priests and prophets. May we become more like Samuel and less like Eli. Give us knowledge, and understanding, and wisdom. May we use our minds. May we look for more good and acquire more wisdom and foresight.

Amen!

January 31

Dear God,

May we become bearers of Good News. May we seek to encourage the down and out. May we reach up to you. May we direct others toward improvement in doing good. May we support the leaders among us. Help us to find ourselves and to help others to find themselves. Help us to redeem the fallen and to direct the lost. May we humble ourselves enough to learn what is best and what is relevant. May we repent when wrong. May we face reality and show ourselves to be honest and trustworthy. May your will become our will. May we be healthy, wealthy, and wise. May we seek the same for others.

Amen!

# February

February 1

Dear God,

May we represent the bearers of Good News. Thank you for all our fellow preachers of the true Gospel of Christ. May we be a fellowship of men and women who bear news of redemption and stability. Help us to promote what is good, right, and true. Help us to do what is relevant for the occasion. May we never bore others with messages that do not meet their needs. May we be careful listeners. May we speak loud enough to be heard and clear enough to be understood. May we preach Jesus as the revelation of your goodness and truth. May we reveal you by word and deed.

Amen!

February 2

Dear God,

Thank you for giving us joy for spreading good news. Help me to be courageous and enthusiastic when telling what Jesus and his followers do for us. Help me to do good, to live right, and to covey truth. May I reveal your loving kindness, mercy, and compassion, so that fellowship and a sense of well-being may be enhanced for many of us. May the life I live, the thoughts I have, and the message I bear serve your redemptive purpose and result in many of us having more abundant lives.

Amen!

February 3

Dear God,

May we not put ourselves down, but lift others. Help us to see ourselves as sinners being saved by your grace. May we not think on our faults, but on your virtues. May we overcome evil with good. Help me to show forth your love. Help me to confess my sins, to repent of them, and to accept your forgiveness. May I not live in sin, or let my mind dwell on sin. Help me to live a redemptive life. Help me to help others to become peacemakers that together we may be called your children.

Amen!

February 4

Dear God,

May the love of Christ for us and our love for Christ keep us from doing evil or neglecting to do good. May we serve and love our fellow human beings. May we think, speak, and live so as to bring about abundant life. May my influence make someone healthy, wealthy, or wise. Help me to live as long as I am helpful. May I be an example of good and not evil. Forgive me of my sins. Accept my offerings. Help me to be grateful. May I continue to grow in knowledge, understanding, and wisdom.

Amen!

February 5

Dear God,

Thank you for all the witnesses of Christ. May we hear, understand, and benefit from their testimony. Thank you for men such as Paul of Tarsus. Thank you for his willingness to share his life. Thank you for allowing me to live in this age. May I so live as to make the coming age better. Help me to understand the past, present, and future. Help me to profit from the past, to live richly in the present, and to have hope for a great future. Help me to promote the reign of Christ. May each year bring about more peace, happiness, and prosperity. May we each help to enrich life in our day. Give me strength, hope, and love.

Amen!

February 6

Dear God,

We know that our lives are being expended. Help us to make ourselves useful to you and yours. May what we think, say, and do bear fruit. Help us to know and to do what is helpful.

Forgive our sins and guide us by your Spirit of truth, love, and reality. May we not be fragmented but rather live wholesome lives. Help us to build useful lives on the basis of truth. May we learn and teach what is approved by you. Give us faith and courage. May we be your children—makers of peace.

Amen!

February 7

Dear God,

Help us to face reality, even when it is not pleasant. May we not become discouraged. Help us to await the time of harvest. May we know when the time is right to act or remain quiet. Give us more faith. May we not become anxious.

Enlighten us, inspire us, and guide us. Give us grace to do without what we cannot attain. May we persevere in faith. Help us to accept our responsibilities and take the blame for our mistakes. May we repent when wrong. Help us to know and to do right.

Amen!

February 8

Dear God,

We recognize you as the God of peace and love. May we be your children and become peacemakers who love people of all cultures. Help us to have one people. May we not worship Baals, but recognize you as our God. Help us to understand that we are not to be given special treatment. May we seek for all mankind the blessings we enjoy. Help us to be cheerful givers. May we be happy to pay our share of taxes. Help us to love our enemies and to have good will toward all people. May we teach by example.

Amen!

February 9

Dear God,

We realize that you do not change. We rely on your faithfulness. We know that your laws control our universe. We are thankful. We have learned of your goodness. We accept you for what you are. You have already proven yourself. May we prove ourselves to also be faithful. May we have integrity and also have strength to endure. Give us courage to face our fears. Give us patience to control our anxieties. Give us strength to overcome our weaknesses. Give us knowledge to overcome our ignorance. Give us wisdom to overcome our foolishness. Give us more faith.

Amen!

February 10

Dear God,

You are our creator, our sustainer, and our hope. We want you to be our Lord. Help us to serve you. May we be one people. May we live in peace and work in harmony for the benefit of all. Show us the way to go and guide us on the way. Help us to do good, to rightly relate, and to seek truth. Make us more grateful, and forgive our sins. Reveal your will. Help us to reveal you and to live faithfully. May we influence others and help them to live abundant lives.

Amen!

February 11

Dear God,

Give me today, I pray, the peace that comes with a clear conscience. Help me to so live as to be free of a guilt feeling. Guide me to repent of all wrong and to accept your forgiveness. Heal me of my diseases. Help me to gain knowledge, understanding, and wisdom that I may be honest and discrete. Help me to follow my instincts when I have good will. Be to me as Jesus reveals you both Lord and Saviour. May I live this day as if it would last forever and, yet, realize how uncertain things are. Thank you for your laws that cannot be changed. Help us to face reality and to have good will.

Sincerely, Amen!

February 12

Dear God,

May we hear your messengers of truth. Reveal to us as much of yourself as we are able to receive; but do not overwhelm us. Give us peace. Make us your children. Give us health, wealth, and wisdom. May all we think, say, or do be used to make you known and accepted as you are. May we see ourselves as we are and be neither humiliated nor proud. May we walk in love, do good, be rightly related, and seek truth. Forgive us when we are hostile or false. May we be your servants who serve your people and do your will.

Amen!

February 13

Dear God,

May we hear your message. May we know your purpose. May we do your will. May we receive your blessings. May we be enriched. May we enrich others. May we learn your truth and use your truth. May we not be merely quoters of your truth, but examples. May others see our good works and know that we are your children. May all we do enhance life by promoting peace and prosperity. May we lead no one astray or hinder anyone's progress. May our thoughts, words, and deeds reveal your Spirit. Thank you for your guidance.

Amen!

February 14

Dear God,

Help me to live sincerely every day. Help me to have integrity. May I speak truth and bear truth by living right. May I live prayerfully. Guide me, encourage me, judge me, and show me mercy. Forgive my sins and help me to be grateful. Teach me to help others. Help me to select good seeds and to lay firm foundations. Give me more knowledge, better understanding, and wiser counsel. Give me peace and joy. Help me to be healthy and wise, and to live more and more abundantly. May I manifest your love. May I so live as to make you known. Make my life redemptive.

Amen!

February 15

Dear God,

Help us to do much good. Help us to properly relate to others. Help us to think straight. Help us to learn truth and speak truth. Help us to promote peace. Help us to experience joy. Help us to share love. Help us to inspire courage. Help us to repent of sin. Help us to accept your forgiveness. Help us to learn from the past. Help us to live in the present. Help us to have hope. Help us to sit erect. Help us to stand firm. Help us to walk straight. Give us patience, stamina, and energy. Be our companion, Guide, and Lord. Give us abundant life.

Amen!

February 16

Dear God,

May we experience faith that would help us to rise up and overcome our sins. May it not be said of us, "They are dead in trespasses and sins." We have learned that knowledge of your goodness and mercy helps us to overcome. May each of us come to such faith as would grow until it would remove mountains. May we know truth and be set free from all that would enslave us. May we become peacemakers, who as your children can help many to overcome ignorance, superstition, and deception. May we know your good ness, righteousness, and truth.

Amen!

February 17

Dear God,

Help us to rise above sin and to make it our goal to partake of what is right. May we accept the principles of Jesus and have revealed to us, "The way, the truth, and the light." May the lost believe in truth and be saved. Help us to believe in truth or principles that live forever. May w see the truth or as we say, "Face the reality." May we remember, as said by Longfellow, "Life is real...." May we accept the "real" and not by deceived by much that comes by "reel," as play-acting. May we be serious, or as we say prayerful.

Amen!

February 18

Dear God,

May we not only rise up and seek to overcome negatives, but also seek what is good, right, and true. May we go about revealing truth so that all whom we influence may live more abundantly. May we go where we should go and do what we should do. Forgive us when we repent of wrong and bless us when we do right. May our faith save us from adversity. May we be to others examples of faith that saves the lost, and we be such peacemakers as to be called, "children of God." May we not hinder good or promote evil. We pray in the character of Jesus.

Amen!


February 19

Dear God,

May we repent and be forgiven and become the reflectors of your light. May your goodness, righteousness, and truth shine forth through us. May we so live as to make truth known. May we each seek to know more and more truth until we see truth or principles that lighten our path and guide our feet. May we spend our lives helping the lost find their way. May our lives be such as to make your truth, goodness, and mercy known to the age. May those who come to know us know you also. May we make you known.

Amen!


February 20

Dear God,

Help us to have vision to see where we are to go. Give us the will to go. May we not linger. May we know that in following Jesus we are moving toward or within your Kingdom or will. May we see your Kingdom of good, righteousness, truth, and justice. Help us to have faith like unto Abraham. May we move away from those who would continue to worship or attribute worth to idols. May we not be deceived but discoverers of truth. We believe in Jesus. Our experiences verify what he reveals. May we show forth our faith as long as we live. Forgive our sins and enrich our lives. May your truth be revealed.

Amen!

February 21

Dear God,

You have given me a mind to think with, hands to work with, and feet on which to travel. You have shown us the way, given us truth, and enlightened our path. You have shown us your will and your purpose. We believe that it is our mission to enrich life. Help us to accomplish your purposes in our time. May we live each day so as to redeem what is lost. May we so live as to help many become healthier, wealthier, and wiser. Bless us that we may bless. Accept our gratitude. Forgive our sins.

Amen!

February 22

Dear God,

Help us to prove all things and to hold fast to that which is good. May we acquire accurate knowledge, adequate understanding, and practical wisdom. May we have a spirit of wholeness. May we live in harmony. Give us this day what is relevant for this day. Give us hope for a better tomorrow. Help us to learn so that we may teach. Inspire us that we may inspire. Help us to give that we may receive. Help us to grow in grace, wisdom, and in stature. May we live so as to be in harmony with others. Deliver us from ignorance, superstition, falsehood, and deceit. Give us truth, vision, insight, courage, and hope. Forgive our sins. Guide us. Keep us.

Amen!

February 23

Dear God,

May we follow Jesus and minister to others rather than demanding others to minister unto us. Help us to attain greatness by serving humanity rather than trying to manipulate and exploit others. Help us to face reality and to be faithful in doing so. Help us to remember that life is reciprocal. May we not try to work aginst reality; may we never work against reality. Help us to know truth and to accept truth. Help us to properly relate to others. May all we do be helpful to all concerned.

Amen!

February 24

Dear God,

As followers of Jesus Christ, we desire to be useful. We know
that it is in giving ourselves in service to humanity, that we really
live. Since we believe that life is reciprocal, we believe in showing
our love for one another. We have learned that Jesus teaches truth.
We believe in Jesus. We believe that all of life is controlled by your
unchanging laws and that Jesus is the personification of those laws.
We have found that it is wise and helpful to face reality and that
our intelligence is our greatest asset. Guide us we pray.
Amen!

February 25

Dear God,

Help us to grow in knowledge, understanding, and wisdom.
May we be human beings that learn and not mere worms that
squirm. We believe that the more truth we know, the more Godly
we are. We have learned that wise people are spiritual people who
control the material and physical. We have also learned that those
people who are externally controlled people are not wise. Help us
to have wisdom to control the physical and material and not to be
controlled by them. We know you as the perfect knowledge and
wisdom that we seek. Teach us that we may know you better.
Forgive our sins.
Amen!

February 26

Dear God,

Help us to discern truth as Jesus reveals truth. Give us the water
of life. May we appreciate Jesus as the fountain of life. Let truth
from Jesus flow through us. Is it not through truth that we are
saved from folly? Is not the fountain of truth the Saviour? Help us
to accept the revelation of Jesus. May we so love that we become
true peacemakers who will be called children of God. Give us
peace and help us to prosper in the building of your Kingdom. May
we seek truth and love one another. May we do good.
Amen!

February 27

Dear God,

Give us the water of life. Quench our thirst, cleanse us from sin. Let us dwell together in unity. May we love everybody. May we ultimately see ourselves as one people with one God. May our goal be to follow Jesus and in so doing bring about a more abundant life for every human being.

We believe that the water of life is a leveling process. It is a cleansing power. It cleans. It quenches thirst. It lifts all boats. Baptize us with that living water. Give us that love that unites that we may all have peace and prosperity.

Amen!

February 28

Dear God,

Help us to follow Jesus and become true peacemakers. May we become your children. Help us to overcome the selfishness of sin. Help us to be united in bonds of peace. Help us as believers in Jesus to show wherein he is "The Author of life and the prince of peace." May we fight not against people, but against sin. May we redeem the lost. Help us to see all humanity as our people. May we carry our load and help others to carry theirs. May we reveal your good will or *agape* to all people. Forgive us and guide us. May we all live more abundantly.

Amen!

February 29

Dear God,

Give us real vision. May we see things as they are. Remove from our eyes the beams that keep us from seeing clearly. Help us to have insight. May we have knowledge, understanding, and wisdom to interpret what we see and experience. Help us to overcome all superstition, falsehood, and ill will. May we face reality and take responsibility for our behavior. May we choose what is good, right, and true. May we live in peace and help one another to become healthier, wealthier, and wiser. May we all live more abundantly.

Amen!

# March

Dear God,

May we show our love for Jesus by doing as he commands us. May we be in harmony with God as Jesus reveals him to us. Become real to us and help us to have integrity. May we seek truth until we find truth. May we be honest and sincere in all our experiences. Help us to be realistic and open. May our love be redemptive. May we be our best selves and allow others to be themselves. Guide us as we go forward. Help us to repent of mistakes. Give us what we need. Use us in your service. Give us more faith.

Amen!

Dear God,

Thank you for Simon Peter. May each us have love and faith that will stand. Help us to be faithful members of the true church, which Peter led. When Jesus confirms our faith and love, may we stand firmly. May we have the boldness to speak truth. May we have the wisdom to speak or remain quiet as the occasion demands.

Help us to apply our minds to gaining wisdom. May we be wise as serpents and peaceful as doves. Help us to promote peace with courage and wisdom. May we do all in our power to avoid falsehood and strife. Give us good will.

Amen!

Dear God,

Give us spiritual food and help us to share it wisely. May we properly nourish those who follow us. May the "Lamb of God" be our example. May the Spirit of love, truth, righteousness, and goodness be our guide. Help us to have integrity and to bear much fruit. May we be quick to learn, slow to speak, and consistent in service. May we repent when wrong. May we accept your forgiveness and move onward and upward. May we build wisely on good, firm foundations. May we sow good seeds, grow good produce, and harvest in due season. May we share the increase. Give us more faith.

Amen!

March 4

Dear God,

May we not be moved by ill will, falsehood, and deceit. May we be committed unto death to do the will of God. May we worship you and you only. May we know you through revelation of truth. May we follow Jesus and reveal you to many. Give us this day all we need and help us to use it wisely. Give us a sense of stewardship. May we, along with our fellow beings, live abundant lives. May we be wise examples of good teaching. Help us to continue to learn new and better ways. May we promote good and shun evil. Let your love flow through us.

Amen!

March 5

Dear God,

Thank you for men, like Paul, who are faithful unto the end. May we all be inspired by his life and teachings. Give us more knowledge, better understanding, and more wisdom. Thank you for grace, mercy, and compassion. Give us a desire to learn. Help us to know truth, to do good, and to live in harmony. May we work with skill and enthusiasm. May we use wisely all that we possess. May we live by faith, wear white robes, and be filled with hope. May we have malice toward no one. May we shun evil and show good will. Forgive our sins. Make us grateful.

Amen!

March 6

Dear God,

Help me today to face the realities of life. Help me to be patient in learning. Help me to be willing to go through normal processes. Help me to comply with all the laws. May my serious thoughts help me to find and do your will. Help me to concentrate. Help me to understand what I experience. Teach me truth. Help me to overcome ignorance, superstition, and falsehood. Give me wisdom that I may live a more abundant life. Help me to teach others to live more abundantly. Help me to maintain good health. Forgive me of my sins and help me to show gratitude. Give me more faith.

Amen!

March 7

Dear God,

Help us to be aware of sin and to overcome all temptation. Help us to be free to invest our lives in doing good, living righteously, and seeking truth. May the whole truth, unvarnished, be our authority. Help us to sow what we would like to reap. Help us to build on firm foundations. Give us vision to see what lies ahead. Help us to prove all things and to hold to what is good, that we may live by faith. Save us from wishful thinking and foolish speech. May we be faithful in pursuing truth.

Amen!

March 8

Dear God,

May we be willing to die doing what we believe to be right. May we exercise true faith without pretense or public show. Be with us as we seriously seek after truth. May we live pure and whole lives without concern for success. Help us to know that we reap what we sow. May we have faith to await the time of harvest. May we patiently endure hardships or inconveniences. May we always be liberal and progressive. Help us to overcome greed and self-centeredness. Give us grace and help us to have poise. Forgive our sins.

Amen!

March 9

Dear God,

Help us to be loyal to truth. May we not seek deception. Help us to accept ourselves and seek to understand others. May we accept responsibility and be aware of opportunities to help others. Give us a sense of belonging. May we learn to love others as you love us. May we love even our worst enemies. May we do good to them that hate us. Help us to make or restore peace. May others come to see us as part of your family. May our loyalty to you as what is real or true take precedence over all other loyalties. Enlighten us and protect us we pray. May we be truly yours.

Amen!

March 10

Dear God,

Help me to know truth. Help me to apply myself to learning.
Help me to gain knowledge, understanding, and wisdom. Help
me to grow in grace and liberality. Help me to share all that is
good, right, and true. Help me to have good will toward all—all
people, places, and things. Help me to grow physically, mentally, socially, and spiritually. May my life be a blessing to
others. Help me to prove all things and to hold to what is good.
May I come to know what, where, how, when, and why and also
who and for whom. Make a man out of me! Help me to remind
people of Jesus!

Amen!

March 11

Dear God,

Give me a vision of reality. Deliver me from ignorance, superstition, and falsehood. Show me the way to go. May your Son be
my example, and your Spirit my guide. Lead on!

May your perfection be my inspiration. Help me to repent when
wrong, and to have self-confidence when right. May my thoughts
and actions be approved by your truth. May I not be deceived.
Help me to be humble. May I have a desire to learn and the will
to learn. Help me to obey your laws that I may bring glory to your
name. Help me to be generous and grateful.

Amen!

March 12

Dear God,

May we, like Peter, leave all sin behind and follow Jesus. May
each of us give our lives in sharing what is good, right, and true.
May your sovereignty be made known. Show us your true self.
May we experience truth and share it. Be with all of us and help us
to know you. Forgive us when we repent of sin. Give us more
vision, may we move forward as we journey through life. Give us
good traveling companions. May we have perfect fellowship. Give
us peace, health, and prosperity.

Amen!

March 13

Dear God,

Help us to show our love by sharing our blessings. Help us to love as Jesus loves and to give as Jesus gives. Thank you for life. Help us to live. Make this day a blessing. Help us to enjoy living today. May we not waste time or energy. Give us strength. Open the doors of opportunity. May we discern truth and be enlightened. Help us to have integrity. May we grow toward maturity. Help us to have wisdom and to inspire more wisdom. Show us the way to live. Forgive our sins as we forgive others. Reveal yourself to us. May we reveal you to others.

Amen!

March 14

Dear God,

We believe that your laws control us. Help us to accept and obey your laws. Give us truth that sets us free. May we be free of sin and live abundantly. Help us to prove what is right that we may have faith to live by. May we overcome all ignorance, superstition, and falsehood, and ill will. Teach us to love one another that we may have peace, prosperity, and a harmonious life. May we see from their point of view. May we give that we may receive, and love that we may be loved. May we repent of all sin and forgive all who repent of sin against us. Guide us through this day.

Amen!

March 15

Dear God,

Help us to follow Jesus in doing what we believe to be right. May we follow, even, when we face danger. Give us wisdom to know when we have gone astray. May we overcome our fears and do what wisdom guides us to do. May we not pursue courses that would destroy our lives. May we have the common sense or wisdom that would keep us from destroying ourselves or our possessions. May we choose to do right. Show us the way of stewardship. Help us to stay healthy, to prosper, and be wise.

Amen!

March 16

Dear God,

Help us to pattern our lives after Jesus, the Christ. May we learn the truth that we may be free. May we think, speak, and act on the reality or truth at hand. Help us to be honest and sincere. May we not be deceived by ourselves or others. Help us to make ultimate truth our God. May we accept no other authority. May we be loyal to Christ as the revealer of ultimate truth. Help us to move forward and upward. May we be true learners and learners of truth. Help us to learn and to teach others to learn. May we respect truth as God or Lord of our lives. Show us the way of life.

Amen!

March 17

Dear God,

May we study and learn until we are in harmony with truth. May we become more and more Godly. Help us to know you as reality or truth. May we flee from whatever would deceive. May we follow the truth or God ahead of us and put Satan or falsehood and deceit behind us. Help us to so live that we will reveal God or truth and destroy Satan or deception. Help us to remain sane enough to face truth. Give us more proof of truth that we may have more faith. Help us to be numbered among the righteous who live by faith. Give us more faith.

Amen!

March 18

Dear God,

Help us to live more wholesome lives. May our goal be integrity or Holiness. Help us to prove what is wholesome and to seek to be whole. May our thoughts, words, and actions reveal truth. Help us to walk with Jesus as He shows us the way of truth that we may truly live. If we are dead in sin, may we be resurrected to a new life. May we repent of all wrong. Help us to know reality or truth. May we accept the God of reality or truth. May we, "Be not deceived for we will reap what we sow."

Amen!

March 19

Dear God,

Give us faith that we may face the unknown future with courage. May our faith remind people of Abraham. May we know God as that reality that provides. Help us to see that truth will prevail. Help us to live in harmony with the never changing laws of God. Help us to see the futility of falsehood. May we turn our faces to God and our backs to Satan. If we are born to or in deceit, help us to be born again. Give us a life of truth. Baptize us in the character of truth. May we have the Spirit of Truth as our father and our brother. Amen!

March 20

Dear God,

We believe that you are light and that you reveal yourself. We believe that you are good, right, and true. Help us to so live that we have nothing to hide. May our love for truth, righteousness, and good be revealed so as to make you known. Help us to promote, educate, and proclaim until we have made truth known. May the "Awakening light of God show us among those who love our fellowmen and thus receive your blessings." May we see truth in our foresight not just in hindsight. Give us more faith and more vision. Amen!

March 21

Dear God,

Help us to give our lives to your will that we may be as crucified with Christ. May we have died to sin and be walking in truth. Help us to wear robes of righteousness. May our meditations, words, and actions be in accordance with truth. May we repent of all deceptiveness and be conveyors of truth. Help us to face life with integrity. May we not deceive or be deceived. May we resist or flee from deception. Give us that life that is lasting. Help us to be free. May our lives be enriched. Help us to know the Christ that saves from sin. May we not miss the mark. Amen!

March 22

Dear God,

   May we learn to understand the truths of life. Help us to learn to learn. May we acquire a liberal education. May we become wise. Help us to share what is good and to repent of any wrong. Help us to make truth known and accepted. Help us to shun the appearance of evil. May we walk by faith as we seek to learn and to do what is good for all concerned. May we teach truth by word and deed. Increase our own faith.

Amen!


March 23

Dear God,

   Help us to live in unity. May we be united in bonds of peace. Help us to love and be loved. Give us graceful Spirits. May we show compassion and mercy. Help us to have self-confidence. May we be bold in proclaiming truth. May we repent of wrong, and may we learn from our mistakes. Enlighten our minds. May we be slow to speak but quick to hear. May we prove all things lest we stumble in ignorance, superstition, or falsehood. May we experience an abundance of faith, hope and love.

Amen!


March 24

Dear God,

   May our self-centeredness be replaced with a spirit of generosity. Help us to see not evil, hear not evil, and do not evil. May we be baptized with good. May our lives prove to be a trinity of goodness, righteousness, and truth. May we have communion with good, fellowship with truth, and a Spirit of love. May our bodies be nourished with good food, clean air, and pure water. May we be strong, healthy and wise. May we live each day without anxiety. Restore our souls with peace and rest.

Amen!

March 25

Dear God,

May we always be friends of Jesus our Lord. May we partake of his life and be as a bride who is closer than a brother. May we be committed to love and honor him as long as we live. May we each day come to know him better and to love him more and more. May we listen to his words and follow his example. May we serve Jesus as we accept the guidance of his Spirit. May our service with him and through him make eternal truth known to the world. May we with Jesus live redemptive lives. In Jesus character we pray.

Amen!

March 26

Dear God,

May we have the vision of the true and beautiful that comes with a clear mind. Open our minds that we may face the truth and be honest and sincere. May we see the trends and be as prophets who sense what is right. May we help others to face reality. Help each of us to be sincere and avoid deception. Help us to build on firm foundations and to sow good seeds. Help us to think clearly and act wisely. May we live in the eternal Present.

Amen!

March 27

Dear God,

Help us to see beyond the present. May we live today so as to make tomorrow a better day. Help us to realize that time is a concept of changes based on the movement of the Earth. Since we live on Earth, may we use our time wisely. May we live in the present, profit from the past, and have hope. May we not turn back or refuse to learn. Today is when we love and work. May we work with patience not with anxiety. May we never fret because of evil-doers. May we be examples of good rather than judges of evil.

Amen!

March 28

Dear God,

Help us to teach and to make learners. May we help others to know that "yesterday died last night, and tomorrow has not been born." We live now or never. To try to project life into the future is to waste it. "If you waste your time thinking and talking about the unknown, you are no earthly good." God is in the reality of the present. God's eternity is now. There is no time with God. "With God a day is as a thousand years." God is the "I am." God is the God of the living. "Death separates us from God." Be with us, we pray.

Amen!

March 29

Dear God,

Help us to be sane, sober, alert, and ready for whatever reality or truth. May we continue to seek knowledge, understanding, and wisdom. Help us to be wise and to live discretely. May we think, plan, speak, and act maturely. May we have energy, strength, enthusiasm, and vision. May we be free to choose. Help us to do what is good, right, and true. Help us to have self-confidence and good will. May we love one another enough to want to do unto others, as we would have them do unto us. Forgive our sins.

Amen!

March 30

Dear God,

Help us to be alert to our neighbor's needs. Help us to be sincerely concerned about human need. May we offer our help when needed. Help us to be responsible and to teach the immature to be responsible. May we be alert, sincere, and patient. May we be humorous and congenial. May we attract good and repel wrong. Help us to be good stewards of all we possess. Help us to invest time and money wisely. May we help others to acquire health, wealth, and wisdom. Help us to learn and to make learners.

Amen!

March 31

Dear God,

Help us to judge ourselves. May we overcome all hypocrisy, pretense, falsehood, and ill will. Help us to know truth and have faith in God. May we live in peace and be called Children of God. May we mature in our thinking, our speech, and our actions. May we avoid mistakes, but be not ashamed to confess and repent when we are conscious of wrong. Help us to act on the eternal and ever present truth. May we take no part in bearing false witness against our neighbors. May we share the good life. Help us to show our gratitude.

Amen!

# April

April 1

Dear God,

May we be strong physically and alert mentally. May we be sincerely helpful. Give us a sense of beauty. Help us to promote decency and order. May we learn from other living beings. Help us to be wise as serpents, but gentle as doves. Help us to be bold as lions and strong like horses. May we learn much and may all that we learn help us to enrich and extend life. May we grow in grace, show our love, extend our help, and share our hope. Give us more faith.

Amen!

April 2

Dear God,

May we so live as to make truth known. When we utter or write the word "God," may it remind people of all that is true, beautiful, and appealing. May we become aware of and obedient to truth. May we repel all that is false. Help us to be what truth demands. Give us faith to accept liberty and to pursue happiness. May we be our best selves. May we hope for the best, and accept the truth. Help us to be more mature and more responsible. Help us to be a blessing to many. May we be useful and inspiring. Help us to learn and to teach. May we think and act wisely.

Amen!

April 3

Dear God,

Help us to do whatever promotes peace and prosperity. Help us to show wisdom, to do good, and to be faithful. Forgive our sins and help us to be grateful. Help us to understand, to be kind, and to show compassion. Save us from fear and give us courage. May we be good stewards of all we possess. Help us to learn truth and avoid falsehood. May we grow in grace and love. Help us to care for our health and to stay strong. May we grow in favor with all who know us.

Amen!

April 4

Dear God,

Give us the humility that enables us to learn. May we continue to learn and teach by precept and example. May we be true disciples who seek truth. May we face reality and avoid deception. Help us to read, observe, think, meditate, and understand. May the thoughts we have, the words we speak, and the things we do be helpful to us and to others. May we help many to live more abundantly. Give us whatever we need to have in order to do what we need to do.

Amen!

April 5

Dear God,

Thank you for the life and teaching of Jesus. May we follow Jesus in making decisions. Give us wisdom and courage to face reality. Forgive us when we sleep when we should be watchful. Thank you for accepting us when we repent. Thank you for your love and mercy. May we always be grateful for all that Jesus does for us. Thank you for giving us your truth. May we be on guard against traitors and false witnesses. May we follow Jesus as he reveals you to others.

Amen!

April 6

Dear God,

We believe in Jesus Christ. We believe that he reveals truth and reality. May we avoid all deception and abide in truth. May we learn to learn and think. May we hear and see so as to discern truth. May we love others and share your truth with them. Give us more and better understanding that we may have more faith. Help us to prove all things and hold fast to all that is good. May we live by faith and be numbered among the righteous. Guide us and use us we pray.

Amen!

April 7

Dear God,

Help us to refrain from dangerous gossip. May we never betray a confidence. Help us to be, "Wise as serpents, but harmless as doves." Give us courage to uphold our convictions. May we protect our loved ones. Help us to learn more about Jesus and to be faithful to him. May we go about doing good, being righteous, and telling truth. May we be wise in speech and refrain from foolish talk.

Give us more faith, more love, and more hope. Give us energy, enthusiasm, and stamina.

Amen!

April 8

Dear God,

Help us to know truth. Help us to be alert. Help us to prove what is helpful to each person with whom we associate. As we know what is right, may we do what is right. Help us to learn from our mistakes so we will not repeat them. Help us to think, learn, and gain skill. Help us to live more abundant lives. Help us to make our lives richer and our world better. Give us grace, mercy, and compassion. Help us to be examples of good. Give us more faith. Help us to be grateful.

Amen!

April 9

Dear God,

Help us to feel the presence of your Spirit. May our minds be open and our thoughts be pure. May we see the hand of Jesus and experience the power of his resurrection. May we recall the life and teaching of Jesus as we journey from place to place. May we bear witness that we have been with him.

May we listen carefully and speak truthfully. May we know and understand what is real and what is false. Deliver us from evil people who try to deceive. May we be free from need and greed. Amen!

April 10

Dear God,

Help us to be as new creatures having been born of the Spirit of God. May we overcome bad habits by doing good.

May we no longer be dominated by the flesh. May we use our minds. May we think and choose. May our minds be open to truth. May we seek more knowledge, understanding, and wisdom. May we see the needs of our fellow beings. May we acquire faith and live by faith lest we be manipulated and tossed about. May we develop character like that of Jesus. Amen!

April 11

Dear God,

We thank you for Jesus. We thank you for sending us an example to follow that has proven to be trustworthy in every way. We know that Jesus is all that we could hope for or seek after. Give us more knowledge, understanding, and wisdom that we may be more like him. May we, like Jesus, be willing and able to meet human need. May we have love or good will toward all your creation. May we have mercy and compassion. May we have skill and zeal as we minister to others. Amen!

April 12

Dear God,

May we be separated from sin and united with you. May we seek to bring about your will or dominion. May we be dead to sin and alive unto righteousness. May we do good, live right, and seek truth. May we follow Jesus and be examples of truth and good will. May we learn and make learners. May our thoughts, meditations, and speech inspire right living. May all that we share be helpful to others. May we become good and faithful stewards. Forgive our sins and help us to show gratitude. Guide us.

Amen!

April 13

Dear God,

Give us peace and rest. May we trust in Jesus and our burdens be lightened. Give us more wisdom. May we do what we can to enrich life and promote freedom. May we be called your children for our efforts to promote peace. May we teach others how to share your love and your peace. May we help to overcome and prevent strife. Help us to promote the welfare and enrichment of all humanity. May we hasten the day when we will treat our fellow human beings as we like to be treated. May we be willing to die rather than kill. Help us to be free of disease. May we be strong and healthy. Inspire us.

Amen!

April 14

Dear God,

May we be united with Jesus. May he be to us the way, the truth, and the light. May he reveal to us what is truth. May we believe in Jesus and overcome our ignorance, superstitions, and false views. Help us to prove what is good and live by faith. May we reflect the light of Jesus and share his wisdom. We thank you for life, liberty, and the right to pursue happiness. May we be good citizens of your kingdom and of our country. Help us to love others as we live this day. Give us hope for tomorrow. In the name of Jesus.

Amen!

April 15

Dear God,

Help us to see what is worthy of worship. May we never bow to graven images. May we seek living truth as our authority. Help us to avoid what is false or pretentious. May we not bow to helpless objects. Give us the wisdom to know what is real and what is false. May we be not deceived. May we not deceive. Help us to know and obey your laws. May we follow the example of Jesus and help others to live abundant lives. Help us to promote peace, happiness, and prosperity.

Amen!

April 16

Dear God,

We believe that Jesus and his teachings will enlighten the world. The need of all people is to know truth and to obey the laws of God. Jesus reveals to us the truth that we might face the realities of life. Thank you for the laws that make things work together for our benefit. We have learned that your laws are dependable. We have come to understand that we reap what we sow and our deeds determine our destiny. Help us to know and to do what is best for each and all of us. May we prove what is good. May we shun what is false and evil. Help us to be true.

Amen!

April 17

Dear God,

May we have faith as Peter. May we seek to be with Jesus. Help us to work together in unity. Help us to live in harmony. Help us to be one humanity serving one God. Help us to seek for a consensus of agreement when we work together. May we never be as a divided house. We know that knowing truth will lead to harmony. We also know that lack of truth leads to division. When we have a mission to fulfill, we need the Spirit of wholeness as a guide. We need the kind of unity that the Disciples experienced at Pentecost when they reached a consensus. Forgive our selfish ways and help us to respect each other.

Amen!

April 18

Dear God,

May my response to your call be, "Here am I send me." Help me to know and understand that I may make wise decisions.

May my will and our will be your will. May we live in harmony with others and all live in harmony under one flag. Help us to do good, love mercy, and walk humbly with you. May we all come to see that our own selfish desires are our worst enemy. Help each of us to see that the Holy Spirit is a necessary guide lest we work against one another. May we have true fellowship in which we have perfect unity.

Amen!

April 19

Dear God,

Help us to see that in unity there is strength. May we as individuals seek integrity and as groups seek unity. May we be unified in mind or Spirit. Help us to find consensus by sharing our thoughts lest we submit to manipulation. May we live as a democracy in which we each feel free to think and act. May our thoughts and actions be in harmony with others. May we surrender any selfish desires that prevent unity of purpose. Guide us by your Spirit of wholeness. Help us to have a richer fellowship and to live more abundantly.

Amen!

April 20

Dear God,

Help us to see that we are individuals capable of unity. May we do what is mutually helpful. May we move toward one God, one Spirit, one people moving toward perfect harmony. May we be led by your Spirit and your revelation of truth. May your purpose be our purpose and your will our will. Help us to overcome ignorance, superstition, falsehood, and ill will. Give us knowledge, understanding, and wisdom. May we show *agape* or good will toward all people, even our enemies. Forgive our sins. Help us to show gratitude.

Amen!

April 21

Dear God,

Help me to see Jesus as Lord of my life. May I see you through him. May he reveal your love to me and help me to reveal your love to others. May we have your peace that we may be of mutual help to one another. Forgive our sins and help us to forgive. Help us to be good stewards. Give us more humility that we may learn, understand, and be wise. Give us energy, enthusiasm, strength, and stamina. Open our eyes and ears. Help us to control our tongues. May we think, speak, and act discretely. Guide us we pray.

Amen!

April 22

Dear God,

May we accept you as you are. May we accept truth and reject falsehood. May we obey your laws that we may receive your blessings. May we be blessed and be a blessing. Help us to experience your love and to love one another. May we have character like that of Jesus whom we recognize as Lord. May we bear witness to truth by word and deed. Help us to sow what we would reap. Help us to be to others what we would have others be to us. Help us to be able, alert, and observing. Help us to be wise. May we experience peace and joy.

Amen!

April 23

Dear God,

Help me to work in your vineyard. May I do what is right as I serve you. Forgive me of my sins. Guide me by your Spirit of wholeness. May what I think, say, and do be acceptable to you. Give me more knowledge, more and better understanding, and true wisdom. Help me to know what is good and to do what is good. Give me more faith. May I take the initiative in doing right and shunning evil. Help me to be a good steward. May all that I do be helpful to all concerned.

Amen!

April 24

Dear God,

Help us to know truth. May we learn to know and to understand. May we have the wisdom to discern truth. Help us to experience love. Help us to reject falsehood and ill will.

May we live in peace and harmony. May we do good, live right, and express truth. Help us to reveal truth and show love to others. May we be good stewards of all that we possess. May we know God and worship him. May we reject all idols. Help us to believe in one God and one humanity. Forgive our sins. Guide and protect us.

Amen!

April 25

Dear God,

Help us to be alert to opportunities to serve. May we be instant to notice these opportunities. May we constantly have good will toward all people. Help us to know good and to do good. May we live in peace and harmony. Help us to bring about what we seek after. May we gain more knowledge, more and better understanding, and may we be given true wisdom. Help us to be careful what we think, say, and do. May we make good covenants and keep all our promises. Guide us into better and better relationships. Forgive our sins.

Amen.

April 26

Dear God,

May we understand the seriousness of our commitments. Help us to give unto you our best gifts. Accept our sacrifices and approve of our plans. Guide us as we make decisions. May we see you as you are and render unto you what belongs to you. Help us to be good citizens of our community, our state, and our nation. Help us to select the best leaders for our people. May we select those who will serve all our people without prejudice or partiality. Guide us today.

Amen!

April 27

Dear God,

May we seek what is best for all of us. Help us to live as one people under one God. May we live in unity and move forward and upward. Give us vision of things to come. May we be prepared for whatever happens. Help us to face reality. May we think, see, and act wisely. May we be quick to see and quick to understand, but act with caution. Help us to repent when wrong and to learn from our mistakes. May we so live as to make each today a good day, and each tomorrow a better tomorrow.

Amen!

April 28

Dear God,

Help us to value each life. May we love our neighbors as ourselves and do unto others as we wish others to do unto us. Give us good will toward all creations. May each of us be blessed and be a blessing. Give us our needs for today. Forgive our sins. Deliver us from evil. May we make you known by showing good will and promoting peace. May we be good examples and teach what is good. May we do good, live right, and seek truth. Be to each of us a guide and companion. May we share your love.

Amen!

April 29

Dear God,

We thank you for all that we are, all that we have, and all that we hope for. Give us more faith, more wisdom, and more gratitude. May we be good examples, be good stewards, and bear good news. Help us to have good fellowship, to teach, to learn, to inspire, and to be inspired.

Help us to know and choose what is right. May we know and shun what is wrong. Help us to be responsible. May we not blame others for our lack and wrongdoing. Help us to be humble.

Amen!

Dear God,

May we learn obedience through our long-suffering. Help us to be kind, merciful, and compassionate. May we have a positive attitude even when we think we are mistreated.

Give us more grace, more patience, and more wisdom. May we be healthy, wealthy, and wise. May we be liberal in our giving, but conservative in our criticism. May we never be greedy or proud. May we promote peace, harmony, and good will. Help us to realize that life is reciprocal. May we remember that we reap what we sow. Help us to sow good seed on good ground.

Amen!

# May

Dear God,

I believe in your faithfulness, your love, and your goodness. I believe that you are all wise, all powerful, and ever present. Give me more faith. Help me to prove all things and to hold to what is good. May I know where I am going and what I seek after. Help me to know better the one who proclaims himself to be the way, the truth, and the life. Help me to know the right way, the whole truth, and the perfect life. May I make known the one who makes you known.

Amen!

Dear God,

Give me patience to wait for your revelation. Help me to believe in your salvation. Forgive my ignorance, superstition, and false beliefs. May I become one who reaches out with faith. Help me that I may be helpful. Give me an alert mind and a strong body. Help me to make good use of my time. Help me to be a blessing to all who know me. Thank you for your help. I approve of all that you do. I hope you can approve of all that I do. I know you are my friend. Help me to know and to do your will.

Amen!

May 3

Dear God,

Help us to be serious thinkers. May we be alert and observing. May we have vision and determination. May we be committed to what is real. Help us to do good, live right, and seek truth. May we think straight and speak clearly. May we shun deception and falsehood of all kinds. Help us to acquire knowledge, understanding, and wisdom. Help us to dwell in peace that we may prosper. Forgive our sins and help us to be grateful. May we be good stewards of all we receive. Guide and protect us.

Amen!

May 4

Dear God,

Give us more faith. May we never shrink from doing good. May we look forward with hope. Help us to endure suffering for doing good. May we keep on doing good and looking forward. May we remember the admonition, "If a task is once begun, never leave it 'til it's done. Be the labor great or small; do it well or not at all." Help us to realize that the harvest lies ahead. We do reap what we sow if we look ahead and faint not. Forgive us for looking back. We know that the Kingdom of Heaven is where we are heading and not where we came from. Give us faith to keep on keeping on. "Sail on. Sail on."

Amen!

May 5

Dear God,

I believe that you hold the future. I want to know you and to make you known. Reveal yourself to me. Give me grace for today and faith for tomorrow. Help me not only to view the goal but also to enjoy the journey. Give me vision. Help me to see ahead. May I move toward the Holy City that is perfect. Give me energy, enthusiasm, and stamina. May I have the will to overcome such hindrances as ignorance, superstition, falsehood, and ill will. Help me to obey your laws and to enjoy your presence. Let me hear your voice and seek your faith. Guide me and give me strength.

Amen!

May 6

Dear God,

Help me to seek freedom and security. May I live by faith. Help me to lay firm foundations upon which to build. Help me to accept Jesus Christ as the way, the truth, and the life. May I have the faith that gives peace, joy, and hope. Help me to see clearly, to understand, and to teach. May I come to know you as Jesus reveals you, and to trust you as Jesus trusts you. Help me to feel at home with those of faith. Forgive me for sinning against you. Help me to be more grateful. Give me today what I need for today. Help me to have hope and be content. Help me to love and share love.

Amen!

May 7

Dear God,

Help us to visualize the results of our plans and actions. May we count the cost and believe in what we are doing. Give us energy, enthusiasm, and determination. May we not waste time, effort, and materials. Give us the joy that comes from seeing the job done well. Help us to do your will and to have your approval.

May we see clearly, hear distinctly, and work diligently. Give us opportunities to learn and help us to learn, understand, and be wise. Give us peace. Enrich our lives.

Amen!

May 8

Dear God,

Thank you for this day. May we rejoice and be glad in it.

Thank you for the revelation of yourself through all that Jesus says and does.

Thank you for life, liberty, and the pursuit of happiness.

May we feel your presence today. Help us to bear in mind that all good comes from you. Thank you for giving us all that we need and have faith to receive. Give us more faith and more patience. Help us to help others to receive your blessings. Forgive our sins and guide us. In Jesus Name.

Amen!

May 9

Dear God,

May we live quiet, confident, and alert lives. Give us the courage of conviction that we may overcome fear. Help us to judge our thoughts, words, and actions. May all that we think, say, and do give evidence that we have been with Jesus. May others see Jesus in us. May we show forth love that is unlimited and peace that passes understanding. May we walk in the right way, speak only truth, and be as light. May we hear you say, "Well done faithful servant." May we experience joy. Amen!

May 10

Dear God,

May we walk the path you have given us to walk. May we climb the steeps you have given us to climb. May we repent of all sins. May we overcome all disease and move onward and upward. May we do what is good. May we relate properly to others, and seek truth. Forgive us when we repent. Guide us in the right direction. Help us to accept responsibility and to share blame. May we not excuse or accuse, but seek what is helpful. Help us avoid or overcome what is false. May we have good will toward all people. Guide us. Your will be done. Amen!

May 11

Dear God,

Help me to live this day a life that shows brotherly love. May others detect that I have been with Jesus. Help me to be mindful of others. May I see clearly and think straight. May my thoughts, words, and deeds be such as would be acceptable to you.

Forgive me of my sins and guide me today. Help me to show gratitude. May I choose what is good. Help me to face reality and shun all falsehood and ill will. Amen!

May 12

Dear God,

Help us to make wise choices. Deliver us from temptations that would destroy our integrity. May we choose to do right. Help us to repent and forgive. May we be made aware of our mistakes.

May we accept Jesus as our teacher and example. Guide us by your Spirit of Truth and good will. Help us to overcome evil with good. May we love our neighbors as ourselves and do, as we would have others do. Give us more faith.

Amen!

May 13

Dear God,

Give us knowledge, understanding, and wisdom. May we repent of all wrong and forgive those who wrong us. Help us to overcome superstition, ill will, and deceit. Help us to prove what is good and to reject evil. Help us to live redemptive lives. May we always face the reality and be aware of pretense. May we never try to get by with wrongdoing.

Help us to accent the positive, and eliminate the negative. May we avoid indecision.

Amen!

May 14

Dear God,

Help us to so live as to remind others of the goodness of God. May we follow Jesus as he reveals what is good, right, and true. May we work toward, ask for, and receive what we need. May we be patient and self-confident. Deliver us from false pride and conceit. May we always be kind and considerate. May we be more generous than greedy. Help us to think, say, and do what builds up. May we be good workers and good citizens. Help us to be grateful.

Amen!

May 15

Dear God,

I realize that all that is good comes from you. I know that you are the giver of life. I thank you for your grace. I know that you give what I need. May I always have faith to receive your gifts. When I seem to lack what I need, give me more faith. Help me to pass on what I receive. May I be a channel of blessing. Help me to be a clean vessel. May my thoughts be clear, my words be kind, and my robes be white. Forgive my sins.

Amen!

May 16

Dear God,

Forgive my sins and help me to live a more abundant life. Help me to be more alert, more sensitive, and more responsive. Help me to relate to others and have a sense of belonging. Help me to find the solutions to my problems without anxiety or strife. Help me to be prepared for the worst but to expect the best. Help me to stay healthy and physically fit. May I have an alert mind. Help me to see and hear. May I not be guilty of sin or ashamed to do good. Live in me.
Amen!

May 17

Dear God,

Help us to understand what we hear, see, and read. May our minds, ears, and eyes be open. May we overcome ignorance, eye, and ear problems. Give us knowledge, understanding, and wisdom that we may choose truth and not be deceived. May we see, hear, and know that God is good, righteous, true, and just. May we come to know what is good, righteous, true, and just. May we accept God wherever we find God and reject falsehood wherever we find falsehood.
Amen!

May 18

Dear God,

May we learn truth from the birds and the flowers as they come and go before our eyes. How much more we need to learn from truths that are fixed. Give us a desire to overcome ignorance, superstition, falsehood, prejudice, injustice, and ill will. May we become more and more like Jesus. May we reach the stage in life where, with Paul, we can say, "To live is to imitate Jesus and to die is better than living a false life." May we have conviction and be willing to die to sin. As our eyes and ears decrease, may our wisdom increase. Guide us today!
Amen!

May 19

Dear God,

Make yourself known to us as reality. You reveal to us principles or laws that govern the universe, which we must obey or perish.

You show us that we are here by your grace. We did not choose to be here. We did not choose our biological parents, our race, our sex, our nationality, or place or time of birth. We cannot be someone else. Help us through love, mercy, and justice to be our best selves.

Amen!

May 20

Dear God,

We have come to know that life itself is reality that exists. We have come to know that truth or reality is the only authority. We cannot do or be anything that is not real. We have learned that the opposite of truth or reality is falsehood. We have learned that what we call "God" has to do with truth or reality. We have learned that in our language we call the false "Satan" which is a synonym for the *devil.* Help us to face reality or God. May we shun Satan or falsehood.

Amen!

May 21

Dear God,

Help us to know you and to trust you. May all our thoughts, our words, and our actions be in harmony with reality. May we never try to do or believe in what is not real. May we not be like evil people who believe in or promote falsehood. May our Lord or dominating force always be truth. May our faith in truth or reality be increased.

Amen!

May 22

Dear God,

May we be whole or Holy. May we not be divided against ourselves. May we prove that which is good, true and of good report. May we have good will, good judgment, and good sense. May we think, speak, and act for the common good. May we examine what we hear as well as what we read. May we not be gullible but seek truth. May we act on proven truth in a faithful and wise manner.

Amen!

May 23

Dear God,

May we maintain our equilibrium. May we face reality without fear or frustration. May we show love, kindness, mercy, and compassion. May we always be our best selves and refrain from being false to anyone. May our thoughts, words, and actions promote sincerity, honesty, and truth. May we show *agape* love or good will toward all humanity. May we be humane. May we continue to grow in knowledge, understanding, and wisdom. May we use all we have, and all that we may receive to reveal truth and avoid falsehood, may we share love and joy, peace and prosperity.

Amen!

May 24

Dear God,

When I get a vision of Jesus and realize how advanced he is for his time, I feel as dead in comparison. I know that when I am at my highest, I am at the feet of Jesus. My wisest acts are as the most foolish of Jesus. May I always remember who Jesus is and that he is trustworthy. I am thankful that I know one who values truth and can always be trusted. I pray that I may continue to hear his voice, as be reveals truth to me.

Amen!

May 25

Dear God,

Help me to face reality. May I grow and multiply as the flocks of Abraham and Lot. Thank you for the room to improve. May I allow others to choose the most fertile pastures. But help me to continue to adjust to reality. May I be aware of approaching dangers. May I have the wisdom to seek higher ground. May I never get so bogged down as to cease making progress. May I never hold too long to the decaying things of the world. Help me to at least move a little onward and upward. Thank you for wise and wealthy elders who can warn us of approaching dangers. Shield us from the foolish.

Amen!

May 26

Dear God,

We look to truth and seek wisdom. May we, like the prophets before us, see things as they are and be able to visualize the future. Give us sight to see, insight to understand, and foresight to determine the future. May we seek wisdom from living history. May we bury the dead. Save us from the evils of our day. May we look forward to better days and better ways. May we advance onward and upward. May we continue to look for new horizons. May we build on the rock solid foundations, and shun the shifting sands as we live in the here and now so as to bless our descendants.

Amen!

May 27

Dear God,

May we tarry where the best institutions are central. May we mingle with teachers and leaders. May we learn to discern truth. Give us courage to oppose all that is false. May we seek to know what works and not be as blind leading the blind. May we have faith based on truth. May we know the truth and not have to trust the unknown. May we seek knowledge, understanding, and wisdom. May we have integrity and grow in grace. Give us more faith.

Amen!

May 28

Dear God,

May I always seek and find truth. May I not be deceived or lulled into accepting something that is false as though it were true. Help me to be an example for the neophyte. May I not sell my birthright for a mess of lentils. May I be controlled by truth or reality. May my mind control my body. May I never allow emotion or sentimentality to rule. Help me to think, know, speak, and act maturely. May I continue to grow in knowledge, understanding, and wisdom.

Amen!

May 29

Dear God,

On the highway of truth I ask many questions, I knock on doors of opportunity, and I seek wisdom to know and act wisely. Give me more proof of truth that I may have more faith. Number me among the righteous who live by faith and among the peacemakers who are called your children. Give me that salvation that comes by trusting in revealed truth. May the truth personified in Jesus rule my life.

Amen!

May 30

Dear God,

Help me to know truth which we call the laws of God. May we not become fools by chasing mirages. Help us to choose truth rather than physical or emotional pleasures as our ruling force. May our minds, not our muscles, be in control. Help us to learn more, to understand better, and to act wiser. Deliver us from the evils of prejudice, superstition, falsehood, and ill will. Help us to be good stewards of good will and fellowship. Help us to share peace and joy.

Amen!

May 31

Dear God,

Help us to obey the only authority, which is truth or reality. May we overcome ignorance, superstition, legalism, literalism, ill will, prejudice, and all other forms of falsehood. Free us from all that enslaves us. May we have the authority which sets us free. May we know the truth.

Save us from our sins. May we believe in the one who personifies truth. May our lives bear witness that we learn from him and that his Spirit of wholeness is our Lord.

Amen!

# June

Dear God,

Thank you for Jesus, our example and teacher. May we, like Jesus, be willing to die to uphold and share truth. May each of us seek to bear our own burdens and to be able to help others bear their burdens. May we enrich life by seeking to give more than we keep. Help us to be mutually helpful. May we never exploit the weak. Help us to compete with our best efforts that we may gain strength. May we realize that the enemy is within. Help us to get rid of our own falsehood. Remove the beam from my eyes. Let me see more.

Amen!

Dear God,

I realize that you are the essence of reality. I also have come to know that facing reality is the only sensible and sane thing to do. Therefore I pray that in any and all situations I will have the intelligence to face reality. I pray that I may learn, understand, and have the wisdom to live by what is real. May I avoid falsehood as one would avoid a deathly plague. May I not receive the wages of sin but receive instead the gift of life.

Amen!

Dear God,

May I be or become a friend of Jesus. May I be the kind of friend that sticks closer than a brother. May I have the greatest of all loves for my friend, Jesus.

May I live for Jesus a life that is true, shunning falsehood in all that I do. May I accept Jesus' revelation of reality, which we call our God. May I always have the desire to learn, which has been called the beginning of wisdom. Guide me into paths of right relationships. May your will be done.

Amen!

June 4

Dear God,

I know that you will always be faithful. Since you are what you are; you cannot not be. You are to me the essence of all that is true. My prayerful or sincere desire is to know you. I want to know what is true. I want to understand what is true. I want the wisdom to live by what is true. I know that missing the mark or being untrue is what is called sin. I pray that my sins may be forgiven. Thank you for Jesus who reveals truth. I believe the acceptance of truth is my salvation. I believe in Jesus.

Amen!

June 5

Dear God,

Today is another day in which to face reality. I pray for the courage to face reality today. I believe the writer who says, "Today is the day of salvation." May I seek truth and shun falsehood throughout this day. May I live today so as to enrich life. Give me more knowledge, better understanding, and true wisdom. May I be discrete in all I think, say, and do. My cup may be small, but I pray that it may be filled with truth.

Amen!

June 6

Dear God,

I pray that I may live an active life. May I not only accept truth, but may I seek after truth. May I think, speak, and act so as to enhance truth. Give me a spirit of wholeness. May I seek the whole truth. Help me to know the truth in all areas of life. May I have a physical body free of disease. May I have an able mind, and a wholesome environment. May I live so as to make my part of the world what I would hope for it be. Give me more faith.

Amen!

June 7

Dear God,

I believe in Jesus Christ. I believe that in the character or name of Jesus lies the hope of the world. May my sincere desires or prayers be that everything with me be done in harmony with the character of Jesus. I believe that Jesus always faces reality. I pray for courage to do likewise. May I have the motto of Herbert Shelton, a follower of Jesus who says, "May the truth prevail, though the heavens fall." I believe in Jesus as the essence of truth.

Amen!

June 8

Dear God,

Thomas Huxley has rightly said that one should do what needs to be done, when it needs to be done, whether he feels like doing it or not. I pray that I will be ruled by my mind or Spirit and not by flesh or emotions. Give me the knowledge to know good and the will to do good.

May I face the realities of life and be a thinker and a doer rather than a wisher and a dreamer. Give me strength and courage. Help me to pursue truth with patience. May I persevere.

Amen!

June 9

Dear God,

Open my eyes that I may see. Remove the beam from my eyes that I may see clearly. May I see life as it is and things as they are. May I come to know and obey the unchangeable laws. Help me to discern truth and to recognize need. Help me to face reality and to avoid deception. May the God of reality lead me. May Satan or falsehood always be behind me. Help me to move away from the falsehood towards truth. May Jesus who, identified or identifies with trust, be my Lord. I recognize the authority of truth. Forgive my ignorance and help me to overcome.

Amen!

June 10

Dear God,

May I find the truth, which I seek after. May I come to know reality. May I think, say, and do what is required of me. Help me to properly relate to other beings, especially human beings. Help me to see and understand the value of completion and unity. Help me to seek holiness or to be whole. May my total being be in harmony with the laws of reality. May I resist temptation. May my mind open to truth and be closed to falsehood. I confess that in ways and at times I fall short or otherwise miss the mark of truth. May I repent and be forgiven.

Amen!

June 11

Dear God,

I accept the invitation of Jesus. May I overcome ignorance, superstition, and all else that is false. May I ask for, seek after, and, at least to some extent, find truth. Help me to gain more knowledge, to better understand, and to think, say, and act wisely. Forgive my sins and help me to be grateful. Help me that I may be helpful. Bless me and make me a blessing. Give to me that I may give to others. Help me to help others to live more abundantly. May we be unified in our efforts to overcome falsehood and disease. Guide us.

Amen!

June 12

Dear God,

May we find your dwelling place. May your home be available to us. Forgive our waywardness. May we no longer follow those who drift to and fro. May we follow only those who are seeking reality or truth. We would be peacemakers. May our seeking peace lead to our being called your children. Be a father to us. Show us the truth. May we be so transformed as to cause others to see that we have been with Jesus. May we reverence truth and be guided by the Spirit of wholeness.

Amen!

June 13

Dear God,

You are the truth or the reality that each of us must face. We are here by your grace. We did not choose to be born. You made provision for us before we were born. Now that we are here, we seek to know your eternal unchanging laws that govern our being. May we know, understand, and obey your laws. Help us to know truth and to overcome all that is false. May we use our minds to search and prove truth. Help us to be faithful in obeying your laws. Give us wisdom and patience. Help us to serve humanity.

Amen!


June 14

Dear God,

May we abide in harmony with you. May we live in harmony with your laws that we may have the gift of life.

May we be your friends. Help us to examine ourselves and to see our weaknesses. May we discipline ourselves until we become transformed into the likeness of Christ. May we, with Jesus as our example, make truth known. Just as Jesus died rather than do wrong or be false, may we be like-minded.

Help us to be peacemakers and life enhancers. May we love our enemies and make them our friends.

Amen!


June 15

Dear God,

We believe the truth that virtues must be added to one another. We pray that we may learn one truth after another and that we will continue to grow in knowledge, understanding, and wisdom. Help us to know more, to understand better, and to think speak, and act wisely. Help us to know what to do and then to do it whether we feel like doing it or not. Help us to live by faith not by wishful thinking. May we seek truth and shun falsehood.

Amen!

June 16

Dear God,

Give us the *agape* type of love that makes us treat others, as we would like to be treated. May we value the life of a friend as we value our own life. Help us to see that we are one humanity and that there is one reality, which we call God. Help us to see that we cannot show greater love than to uphold truth. The truth is that your life to you is what mine is to me. Friends love one another and consider themselves equals. Give us this greatest love.
Amen!

June 17

Dear God,

Help me to refrain from judging without evidence. May I not be deceived by those who gossip without knowledge. Help us to prove what is true and to hold fast to truth. May my thoughts, words, and deeds be helpful to others. Help me to remove the beams from my own eyes. May I come to know that my foe is my own sins. It is my own sins that I repent of. It is my own character that needs to be improved. I am the one that needs to mature. Help me to grow in grace and truth.
Amen!

June 18

Dear God,

May we never get so elated that we refuse to face reality. We realize that at times we feel we can do the impossible. We temporarily follow our emotions or feelings. It may be that we quit thinking and act as though insane. It may be that we are temporarily insane.

The Godly or Spirit-led person is guided by the intellect. Help us to retain our sanity. If we do become temporarily insane, we pray for restoration, lest we act foolish or dangerous. Forgive us for allowing ourselves to be overcome by emotions. May we not be dominated by the flesh.
Amen!

June 19

Dear God,

Like Peter, we need to affirm our faith. We know that real love is not

just some sentimental emotion. Thank you for reminding us to show good will rather than be led by emotions. May we be led by your Spirit of wholeness. Help us to retain our sanity and to have integrity. Help us to contain ourselves when angry or over elated. May we stand on solid ground and not drift too far from the shore.
Amen!

June 20

Dear God,

Like Job, we sometimes face hard trials. Give us more patience and help us to be faithful. May we retain our integrity. Help us to know you and trust you. We know that all things work for our good when we retain our faith and control our feelings. Help us to know the reality or truth and not to be lulled into falsehood by misguided friends. Help us to face life with patience, stability, and good will. Help us to see that the real enemy is falsehood. Give us more faith.
Amen!

June 21

Dear God,

We believe the truth. We are in control of our lives under your unchangeable laws. We are as priestly Kings. No one can force us to sin. We are our own enemies. It is not some external force, but the human ego that gets us in trouble. No one can control our thinking against our will. We each have our own minds. Our minds can be influenced by external forces, but they are controlled from within. We cannot blame others for our sins. We either repent or bear the consequence. Reality does not show favoritism.
Amen!

June 22

Dear God,

Help me to show good will toward every one. May I love my fellow human beings, as I love myself. May I remember to do unto others, as I would like for others to do unto one another. Grant that I may never exploit others so as to take an unfair advantage of them. Help me live in harmony with others of good will. Help me to observe, understand, and teach the law of reciprocity. Help me to be an instrument for dispensing your love.
Amen!

June 23

Dear God,

As a human being, determined to live a life of integrity, living among the just and the unjust, I, like others of integrity, will experience sorrow and grief. I am thankful that our model, Jesus of Nazareth, was such a person. Thank you for his integrity and keen insight. Thank you for a man of sorrows and acquainted with grief, who wanted to save his fellow human being from the evils that lay ahead. Help us each to be more like him. May each of us be an angel of mercy. May we bear good news. May we project truth and good will. Guide us and protect us from evil.

Amen!

June 24

Dear God,

Help us to avoid those who choose to work in the dark because their deeds are evil. We know that those who do evil are afraid of light. May we so live until we are not afraid for others to see our works. Help us to make good known. May we release Jesus in daylight rather than arresting him at night. Give us the courage to face our enemies where they work. Help us to see that our own fears and a spirit of envy and jealousy are our worst enemies. Forgive our sins we pray.

Amen!

June 25

Dear God,

Help us to see Jesus, whom we worship. We thank you that he was willing to die on the tree rather than teach falsehood. His being willing to die for his friends, draws us to him. We pray that we may have the same courage. May we be willing to identify with Jesus. As Jesus bears witness to truth for our benefit, may we bear witness to benefit others. Help us to spread light by revealing truth and facing reality. May we, too, live redemptive lives. May we not be afraid to face death.

Amen!

June 26

Dear God,

Thank you for your grace. We believe that your grace is sufficient to meet all our needs. We know that we did not create ourselves. We are here because of your grace. You have made provision for all that we need. All the necessities of life are available to us. We pray that we will discover and make good use of what you have provided. May we be good stewards of all we may acquire. Give us knowledge, understanding, and wisdom to live discretely.

Amen!


June 27

Dear God,

May we be aware of your presence. We know that in you we have our being. Help us to so live as to make you known. May we be extensions of your love, your goodness, your truth, and your mercy. May others see your life in us. May we extend your grace. May we be peacemakers that would cause us to be called your children. May we receive your blessings and bestow them on others. May we be mutually blessed. Forgive us for not making you better known. Give us more faith.

Amen!


June 28

Dear God,

I pray that I may come to understand, as I am understood. May I acquire knowledge, understanding, and wisdom. Help me to know your laws and to do your will. Help me to be the person that I would like as a friend or neighbor. Help me to be an example that I would like to follow. May I try hard to improve the one I see in the mirror. May I judge myself as I judge others. Forgive my debts as I forgive my debtors. Help me to grow in love, mercy, compassion, and gratitude. Help me to follow Jesus. It is his character that I would like to emulate.

Amen!

June 29

Dear God,

Help me to evaluate the work of my hands. May I cut off the activities that are not helpful to someone in some way.

Give me wisdom to work diligently and discretely. May I have integrity and be coordinated. Help me to gain skill and to persevere in doing what is right. May I do things decently and in order. Help me to be open-minded, congenial, and cooperative. May I enjoy life and enrich others. May I work toward health, wisdom, and prosperity for all my community.

Amen!

June 30

Dear God,

May I develop the wisdom that I need so as to cultivate friends. Help me to reach agreement with others lest they become enemies. Help me to learn diplomacy and to avoid conflict. Help me to know when to stand and when to run. May I do unto others as I expect others to do unto me. May I go a second mile to attain or retain peace. Help me to avoid or prevent anger and conflict. Give me the grace to turn the other cheek. Help me to relate properly to others. Give me humility and wisdom to learn and teach.

Amen!

# July

July 1

Dear God,

May I pay all my honest dues, customs, taxes, and debts. Help me to so live that I may avoid penalties, and fines. Give me foresight and wisdom to avoid imprisonment. May I avoid addictive substances and bad habits. Help me to correct minor mistakes before they cause major problems. Give me a strong will, an alert mind, and a good attitude. Help me to make friends and to enjoy fellowship. Help me to reveal the good, the true, and the right. May others see Jesus in me. In Jesus' name I pray.

Amen!

July 2

Dear God,

Help me put the principles that Jesus taught to work in my life. Help me to follow Jesus in revealing what is good. Help me to see as he saw and to love as he loved. May I have the faith that heals and the grace that forgives. Help me to learn, to teach, and to reveal truth. Help me to overcome ignorance, superstition, and all else that is false and harmful. Help me to put Jesus and what he revealed first in my life.

Amen!

July 3

Dear God,

Help me to face my sins and to overcome them. May I see my own sins for the enemy that they are. May I be always ready to confess and repent of known sins. Forgive me for not recognizing all that is false. Help me to avoid false teaching and to discern truth. Help me to seek your forgiveness. Remind me to remember that Heaven is just a sin away. Cleanse me of my sins, lest I feel unwanted and undone. Give me grace and help me to have more faith. Thank you for your love and mercy.

Amen!

July 4

Dear God,

Help us to accept reality and to make the most of what we are faced with. Help us to be patient in bearing our burdens and in solving our problems. May we not fret about things we cannot change. Give us the knowledge, understanding, and wisdom that we need. May we work together for the benefit of all concerned. Help us to learn from our mistakes and to make corrections when wrong. May we continue to grow and to accept responsibility. May we be grateful.

Amen!

July 5

Dear God,

We commit our way unto you. Help us to live by faith. May we seek to prove what is good, right, and true. Give us more wisdom and help us to use good judgment. Bless our efforts that we may help others to build a good community. May we share a fellowship of joy and peace. May our sincere desires be in harmony with all that promotes abundant living. May we follow in the steps of Jesus. Thank you for your love and mercy. Amen!

July 6

Dear God,

Thank you for showers of blessings. May we absorb your living waters. May we not suffer from dry land and excess heat. Forgive our sins. May we not deserve punishment for wrongdoing. Bless us and make us a blessing. Help us to conserve what is good and to seek what is better. May your Kingdom come and your will be done. Thank you for your divine laws. Help us to obey them. Amen!

July 7

Dear God,

Help us to find and enter the strait gate. May we stay sane and sober lest we walk a crooked path. Help us to be true witnesses of all that is good and true. Give us health and make us strong. May we endure whatever suffering will strengthen us. Give grace and power to live by faith in a just and Holy God. May we so live as to reveal God to the world. May we grow more acceptable each day. Help us to be examples of truth and to overcome falsehood. Amen!

July 8

Dear God,

Thank you for the right to choose. Help us to choose wisely. May our conduct show that we have chosen to serve the Holy One. Help us to reveal your goodness. May we inspire others to make the right choice. Be with us in all that we think, say, and do. May

our faith make us whole. Give us nourishment for the day and forgive our debts. Help us to be of service to others. May we choose what is mutually helpful. Bless our choices.
Amen!

July 9

Dear God,

I realize that you managed quite well before I was born and you will manage when I am gone. I know that I am here because of your grace. In the present, I pray that I may be useful in enriching someone's life. May my thoughts, words, and acts make your love known. I know that your grace is sufficient to meet all our needs. Increase our faith that we may rely on your goodness and mercy. Enlighten our minds. Give us wisdom. Make us useful. Thank you for being you.
Amen!

July 10

Dear God,

Help us to meet under the shelter of your wing. May we have fellowship in your presence. Help us to work together in unity. May we all move toward you. Deliver us from the sins that cause conflict and division. May we learn to communicate until we reach consensus. Help us to appreciate others and to think of one another as of equal value. May we learn to understand and accept our differences. Guide us into paths of righteousness. May we bring glory to you.
Amen!

July 11

Dear God,

May we come to know you as the giver of life. Help us to know, experience, and share the abundant life. May we enrich each other as we make God's love and mercy known.

Help us to love one another and to help one another. May we each give that we may each receive. May we do as we would have others do. May we each understand the law of the harvest. May we each sow and reap. May we bear in mind the truths that we have learned. Give us more truth. Deliver us from falsehood.
Amen!

July 12

Dear God,

May we keep on growing in grace, love, knowledge, understanding, and wisdom until we are mature. May we become more and more like the Christ. Help us to live redemptive lives. May we learn and teach what is right, wholesome, and true. Forgive us for our mistakes. Help us to be examples to those less mature. We thank you for your love, mercy, patience, compassion, and understanding. We thank you for the guidance and comfort of your Holy Spirit.

Amen!

July 13

Dear God,

We thank you for the testimony of those who, like Isaiah, were obedient to your call. Thank you for the great and lovely writings of your prophets. Help each of us to have vision and to respond to whatever you call us to do. May none of us perish for lack of vision. May we see the trends and accept our responsibility. Give us knowledge, understanding, and wisdom to interpret what we see and hear. May we be willing to do what needs to be done. May we feel the nearness of your presence.

Amen!

July 14

Dear God,

Give me patience and understanding. Give me the grace to bear suffering rather than live in conflict. May I overcome evil with good rather than trying to fight evil with more evil. May I be an example of right living. Help me to be a peacemaker. Give me the ability to withstand persecution. Help me to help others in times of distress. Help make to cultivate those who promote peace. Help each of us to apply ourselves to learning. May we be wise as serpents and peaceful as doves.

Amen!

July 15

Dear God,

Thank you for the privilege of living amid diversity. I know that I learn from many. Like Paul, I am debtor to different people. May I find means to pay back those who have helped me. May I be content

only with a debt of love. Help me to show love and gratitude. May my character reflect the character of Jesus. May I go about doing good and spreading good news. Help me to be a good steward of all that I possess. May I be helpful in bringing about abundant living. May I help to make your goodness known. Give me more faith.
Amen!

July 16

Dear God,

Since you give to us what we ask of you, may I have the wisdom to ask for what best meets my needs. Give me the knowledge, understanding, and wisdom to discern what is needed. Thank you for your good will. Thank you for meeting our needs. Give me grace to accept your gifts and wisdom to be a good steward. Help me to use my resources for promoting your Kingdom. Forgive my sins. Help me to give as I receive.
Amen!

July 17

Dear God,

Help me to preach and teach with sincerity. May I persuade with truth. May I not try to deceive with flattery or coercion. Help me to lift high the banner of Christ. May Jesus be seen as the way, the truth, and the life. May I be able to present Jesus as your revelation. May the words of my mouth and my meditations be acceptable to you. May my life, my love, and my works be in your name. May I so live as to be an instrument for good and a channel of blessing.
Amen!

July 18

Dear God,

May I, with Paul, confirm your presence. Who are you and what message do you have for me? What do you bid me to do? Am I persecuting you or promoting you? Am I building your church or am I destroying it? May I bear witness to your saving grace. Help me to turn people from falsehood to truth. Thank you for Paul's conversion. Thank you for his life and work. Thank you for Paul's letters of encouragement. Thank you for the churches Paul helped to build. Help us to repent of sin and to learn and teach.
Amen!

July 19

Dear God,

Help us to do what needs to be done. May we do your will. Reveal to us the way of truth. May we know what is truth. May we turn away from evil unto what is good. Give us more faith, more love, more patience, and more compassion. May we become more like Jesus. May others see that we recognize Jesus as Lord. May we follow Jesus as the way of life and the truth of life. Forgive our sins and accept our gratitude.

Amen!

July 20

Dear God,

May we be guided by your Holy Spirit. May we know and obey your laws. Give us open eyes, open ears, and open minds. May we be seekers and learners. May we learn what is good, right, and true. Give us more knowledge, understanding, and wisdom. Give us the will to do what we know we should do. Help us to make others healthy, wealthy, and wise. Help us to make wise choices so as to promote joy, peace, and prosperity. May we prove all things and hold to only what is good.

Amen!

July 21

Dear God,

May we be grateful for your blessings. May we repent of all sin that would repel your blessings. Give us that unspeakable joy and abiding peace that comes from obedience to your laws. May we overcome pride and remain humble enough to learn and receive. Thank you for love, beauty, and wholesomeness. Thank you for the freedoms we enjoy. May we know the truth that sets us free. May we choose what is good. Forgive us for all our sins, which we confess are too many.

Amen!

July 22

Dear God,

May your will be done. May each of us be set apart as a servant in your Kingdom. We do not know what the future holds, but we pray that it may be the best possible. May each of us be used to do

your will. May each of us become strengthened and enlightened. May our society be as a nation under your guidance where there is malice toward none and liberty and justice for all.
Amen!

July 23

Dear God,

May we be as one body with the Spirit of Jesus Christ in control. May we each work for all. May we each be set apart to do what we can do best. May we work in harmony so as to bring about peace, joy, love, and prosperity for all. May we each learn some skill that will make us useful. May each of us overcome ignorance, superstition, and falsehood. May each of us learn to rightly divide truth. May we be led by your Spirit and not be controlled by our changing emotions.
Amen!

July 24

Dear God,

May each of us learn to be sincere and honest. May our righteousness be real. Forgive us if we yield to the temptations we may face. May we confess and repent of each wrong. May we accept your forgiveness and show our gratitude. May we learn from our mistakes. Help us to grow in knowledge, understanding, and wisdom. May we learn truth and live by faith. May we each learn to be decisive and to accept responsibility. May we avoid manipulation and coercion. Help us to be healthy, wealthy, well-adjusted, maturing individuals.
Amen!

July 25

Dear God,

May we each choose truth and right. May each of us so live as to experience your blessings. May we show our gratitude for each blessing. Help us to profit from the past, make the best of the present, and have hope for the future. May I make the world better. May my influence be beneficial to my people. Give me what I need and help me to be a good steward. May those with whom I live find harmony and peace. May each of us live healthy and useful lives. Guide us we pray.
Amen!

July 26

Dear God,

I am aware that good and evil are matters of the mind. I am controlled by my thoughts. Help me to think clearly and to act decisively. May I seek to know what is good, right, and true. Help me to act with faith and good will. Help me to know what is good and to do what is good. May I never be led astray by my emotions and physical desires. May I learn to know right and act wisely. Help me to choose what is true and to shun what is false. Forgive my sins and help me to be grateful.

Amen!

July 27

Dear God,

Help me to know your will. Give me knowledge, understanding, and wisdom. Help me to see what needs to be done. Help me to accept responsibility and to act as necessary. May I have the guidance of your Holy Spirit of truth and love. Help me to understand and obey your laws. Help me to be helpful to others who have good will. May we work together for mutual benefit. Help each of us to work for the benefit of all of us. Help us to live abundant lives. May I use my influence to make our world a better place.

Amen!

July 28

Dear God,

Help me to be a learner. May I be one of Jesus' followers. Show me the way to go. May I be willing to remain or ship out as were the early disciples. May I fulfill your purpose for my life.

Give me wisdom to know right and courage to do right. Help me to have a strong, healthy body and a well-informed, alert mind. Help me to relate properly to others. May I love my neighbors as myself and do unto them as I wish them to do unto me. Guide me by truth and love.

Amen!

July 29

Dear God,

Help me to face life with courage and determination. Help me to know truth, and help me to make wise choices. May I learn to respond to problems in a positive way. Help me to stay cool, calm, and collected. Give me grace to accept what I cannot change and the ability to improve what can be changed. Give me strength to endure when I must suffer. Help me to sense your presence. May I so live as to grow in grace. Forgive my sins and give me an attitude of gratitude.
Amen!

July 30

Dear God,

Thank you for giving us insight. Thank you for a sense of well-being. May I learn what to expect from others. May I increase in faith and gratitude. Help me to accept responsibility and to appreciate others who do likewise. Help us to live in harmony and to work for mutual benefit. Make us aware of our opportunities and ready to respond to them. Help us to stay healthy, interested, and alert. May I live a long, fruitful life.
Amen

July 31

Dear God,

Help me to learn to do what needs to be done. May I see ahead; may I plan ahead. May I be able to read the signs that direct my path. Give me vision and understanding. May I live and work with purpose.

Be with me as I seek to help others to find their way. May I learn to be a good example, a good guide, and a good teacher. Help me to share what is good and to overcome what is evil. Help me to be a good influence. Thank you for answering my prayers.
Amen!

# August

August 1

Dear God,

Thank you for the truth about Jesus. I believe he is our example. Help me to know him and to follow him. May I learn to know what is right and form a habit of doing what is right. Help me to make wise choices. Help me to be alert and to control my emotions. May I make positive and helpful choices.

Forgive my sins and help me to be grateful. May I learn to use my ability and acquire and develop more and greater ability. Guide me throughout each day.

Amen!

August 2

Dear God,

Help me to endure trials and tribulations that I cannot avoid. May I act wisely and retain a good attitude. May I have courage and patience.

Help me to be a good example. May others see Jesus in me. May I be enlightened and use good judgment. Help me to have self-confidence and self-respect. Help me to know when to stand and when to run. Help me to live so as to have good health and good cheer. Help me to use my time more wisely.

Amen!

August 3

Dear God,

May we who call ourselves Christian, live as those who respect the Holy City. May our lives reflect your holiness. May we try to live wholesome lives. Help us to have integrity. Help us to overcome ignorance, superstition, intolerance, and ill will. Help us to know and follow good examples. Help us to know and to obey your laws. Help us to repent when wrong and to be faithful when right. Give us energy and enthusiasm.

Amen!

August 4

Dear God,

Thank you for choosing us to carry on your work in this world. Thank you for giving us the opportunity to serve you. Forgive us for the wrong choices we have made. Give us knowledge, understanding, and wisdom. Guide us into paths of righteousness. May we be more thoughtful and move careful in the future. Help us to be good stewards. May we seek to know you and to do your will. Help us to develop good habits.

Amen!

August 5

Dear God,

Thank you for the prophets who know you and speak for you.

Thank you for those who have foresight and insight and integrity who speak truth. Help us to examine what we read and to accept truth. May we never be fooled by false prophets who resort to false propaganda.

Thank you for the revelation that comes to us through the life and teaching of Jesus. Help us to know the truth that sets us free from falsehood and ill will.

Amen!

August 6

Dear God,

Thank you for the authority of Jesus. We believe that Jesus speaks truth. We also believe that all authority is truth. Help us to obey truth and to rebel against all falsehood. May we seek truth and not be led astray by our emotions. May we seek good even when we feel bad. Help us to use our intelligence and not be deceived by the works of the flesh. Help us to bear the fruits of the spirit. May we obey your laws. Forgive us our debts and help us to be grateful.

Amen!

August 7

Dear God,

I thank you for the young people who follow Jesus. May I inspire and teach the young to follow Jesus. May the young be found in your house examining your truth on many occasions.

May our church buildings be as your house. May they be houses of prayer, where we can be healed and in our right mind.

Give me each day what I need to serve you. Help me to know truth and obey your laws. May I help the young to live more abundant lives. Amen!

August 8

Dear God,

May more and more expectant mothers be told by your messengers that their offspring may be a child of God. May your Holy Spirit inspire mothers and children. Help our mothers to look for the best in their children. May the children not have regrets, but be about their Father's work. Help each of us to live as your children. May we be called of Jesus to promote peace and obey truth. Help us to love one another. Thank you for the guidance of your Spirit. Amen!

August 9

Dear God,

Thank you for hearing our prayers. We believe in the Lord Jesus, and we make our prayer in his name. We claim the guidance of your Holy Spirit of truth and love. We believe that all things are for our benefit. We are here to glorify Christ, as Christ came to glorify you. May all that we think, say, and do be acceptable to you. May each of us be helpful in making Jesus known, that you may be our Lord and Redeemer. May we live the abundant life. Amen!

August 10

Dear God,

Thank you for caring for our well being and allowing us to choose. May we choose to learn and to do your will. May we rejoice when right and repent when wrong. May we be humble enough to learn and persistent in attaining truth. May we seek what is right, ask for what is good, and teach what is true. May we accept your revelation and live by faith. Help us to know and follow Jesus Christ. Help us to have integrity and to show forth good will. Amen!

August 11

Dear God,

Give us more and more of yourself. Help us to ascertain more and more truth. May we learn truth until we are able to know that we know, so as to act with knowledge, understanding, and wisdom. Help us to act on our knowledge, understanding, and wisdom, so as to help and not harm all concerned. Help us to start where we are and to learn as much truth as we can and to apply truth as relevant according to need. May we enhance human life. Amen!

August 12

Dear God,

Help us to know truth so that we may have faith. May we learn until we overcome our doubts. May we acquire knowledge, understanding, and wisdom sufficient to deal with our problems and our duties, so as to enhance the life or lives you have given us.

Help us to share our knowledge, understanding, and wisdom any way that we can, so as to help as many needy people as we can. May we help others to help themselves and others. Amen!

August 13

Dear God,

Help us to share truth and good will, so that more and more people will be equipped to have and enjoy peace and plenty. May we be able to in some way reverse the trend of the rich getting too many dollars and the poor getting too few. May we all use our material blessings to promote mental and spiritual growth. Help us to acquire truth and to share it along with good will. May we know that real life is mental. May we not waste time and energy playing useless games. Amen!

August 14

Dear God,

Help us to discipline ourselves and to help others to discipline themselves. Help us to be good examples. May we do as we teach, so the learners can understand true value. May we not be hearers or talkers only. May we have faith so as to act on what we believe. May we ask for truth, seek after truth, and open doors to truth. May we seek truth that reaches bliss or Heaven. May we grow in knowledge, understanding, and wisdom as long as we live. When we die, may our influence live on. May our characters promote or enhance life from generation to generation. May we not be dead because of sin.

Amen!

August 15

Dear God,

Help us to not only be born of flesh, but also to be born of God or truth. We realize that without knowledge, understanding, and wisdom we are mere animals. We appreciate the fact that you are in the flesh but not of it. May we control the flesh and not be controlled by it. Help us to follow Jesus as he reveals truth to us. Help us to reach the place where we will subdue the flesh and exalt the spirit. May we not be driven by sex, food, and drink. May we not only seek the strength of the eagle, but also the peace of the dove.

Amen!

August 16

Dear God,

May we not be stuck in the past, but grounded or founded in truth. May we not seek fun, and damn mentality. May we, rather grow in the grace and knowledge of the great teacher, Jesus, whom we know as Saviour. Help us to know and know we know that we may have faith in God who personifies truth. May we not quote but study and think. A child with little knowledge and almost no wisdom can quote Scripture. Let your Spirit be our guide. May we have more truth and good will to share it.

Amen!

August 17

Dear God,

Help me to do what I need to do, so that I may be useful to myself and others. Help me to be alert to the needs of others. May I think and act in a way that I may be a blessing to many. Lead me in paths of righteousness. May what I do cause people to think and act wisely. Help me to inspire others to discipline themselves. Help me to teach by leading the way. May I never be satisfied to just pass words, but help me to enrich life.

Amen!

August 18

Dear God,

Help me to enrich others by teaching them to find and teach truth. Help me to remain humble enough to love knowledge, understanding, and wisdom. Help me to promote truth, good will, peace, and prosperity. Help me to see what needs to be done and give me the power of truth to do it. May I remember to seek truth for every task. May I never practice the folly of fools. Help me to gain knowledge, understanding, and wisdom and to be numbered among the cheerful givers. May I share what I have.

Amen!

August 19

Dear God,

Help me to continue to seek truth, for I know without truth I cannot live. I know you are truth and love. I also know that to know you is to live and not to know you is to be as dead. Help me to continue to seek truth and to show good will. May I be criticized for knowing and doing good and not for playing the fool. Help me to make those who know me wiser than those who do not know me. May my life advance knowledge, understanding, wisdom, and good will. Forgive me for being more ignorant than wise.

Amen!

August 20

Dear God,

Give me the rest that I need. Help me to know more and more how to work effectively. May I do what needs to be done without overworking.

Help me to repent when wrong and to be firm when right. May I continue to seek truth. May I come to know and to know I know that I may be faithful. Help me to overcome ignorance, superstition, falsehood, and ill will. Help me to be a steward of all I come to possess. Help me to know and follow the principles of Jesus.

Amen!

August 21

Dear God,

I am aware that of the vast knowledge available, I have only a tiny amount; of that I do have, some of it is incomplete. I am not yet dead, and as long as I am sane and alert I will learn. Help me to share with those who have knowledge that we all be enriched.

Help me to, not only have knowledge, but to also have the understanding and wisdom, to be relevant. Help me to teach others by being a faithful servant. I hate ignorance and deception.

Amen!

August 22

Dear God,

I am thankful for what I know I know. May I act on what I know is right. May I acquire more and more truth that I may overcome the evil of ignorance. May I remain neutral when in doubt. May I never harm others because of ignorance of evil, or the evil of ignorance. May I practice self-discipline. Help me to subject my body to my mind. Help me to control my desires, emotions and drives. May I never over-indulge in excitement, food, drink, and sex.

Amen!

August 23

Dear God,

May I take life as I find it and, through examining myself and by thinking and planning, make the best of it. May I keep my thoughts pure and my words clean. Help me to live a life with a future. May I never fail to take a long view. Forgive my weaknesses that are caused by lusts of the flesh and lack of wisdom. May I not only be a learner, but also inspire others to learn. Help me to be grateful, joyous, and happy. Help me to avoid disease, stiffness, and pain. May I share what is true, beautiful, wholesome, loving, and good.

Amen!

August 24

Dear God,

May I have the character that my Son will be happy to reveal. May I pass to my descendants the bread of life–the truth and love that promotes peace and prosperity, rather than a stone of ignorance and evil that would send them to an early grave. May I have the kind of faith that appropriates grace and truth, that enriches life, and makes it last. May I not be deceived or despise truth. May I be your friend and not offend.

Amen!

August 25

Dear God,

May I be added to those earlier learners whom Jesus called the light of the world and the salt of the earth. May I never be a paid killer, but one who is approved of truth to enlighten and preserve. May I hate evil and overcome it with good. May I be like Jesus and be blessed as a peacemaker, rather than be honored as a killer. May all my heroes be peace lovers. Help me to gain truth and prevent strife that leads to early death and hell.

Amen!

August 26

Dear God,

May I accept Jesus of Nazareth, the Prince of peace. May I never accept, Jesus Barrabas, the leader of war. Give me more knowledge, understanding, and wisdom that I may know the difference. May I never beget a son like Barrabas. Help America turn from ignorance and deceit to truth. May we have love, the symbol is the dove. May we have the spirit of truth and love that unites, rather than have hatred that separates. Let us enhance the church and state.

Amen!

August 27

Dear God,

May we so live as to indicate by the way we live our daily lives that we are an enlightened people. May we have knowledge, understanding, and wisdom. May we overcome such enemies as ignorance, superstition, prejudice, perversion, falsehood, ill will, and deceit. May we be wise and not act as fools. May we be prayerful or serious. May even our humor be serious. May we, by our actions, reveal truth and good will to all with whom we associate. May people take note that we are like Jesus.

Amen!

August 28

Dear God,

May the Lord of my life teach me to be wise and not a fool. May I think, talk, and walk with integrity. May my life reveal truth and love. May I be inspiring, not merely an attractor of attention. May I inspire thought and right action. Help me to reveal truth and love by all my influence until death is destroyed. May I live with truth and good will until I no longer have the breath of life.

Amen!

August 29

Dear God,

You reveal yourself to me as The Holy Spirit of truth and love. You have shown us that you approve of Jesus of Nazareth who revealed you to us. Help me to live as Jesus lived so as to continue to make truth and good will known. May I never make deception a way to walk. May I have integrity and remove myself from known evil. May I think more and more of truth and good will until it is my way of life. May I overcome evil with good. May I be what people of truth and good will call Godly.

Amen!

August 30

Dear God,

To me you are the personification of truth and good will. Help me to be your servant and help me to be your friend. May I have faith like the faith of Abram. May I seek to find or make my country into a country made of truth and good will. May its builder and maker be called the Lord God. May truth reign. You have shown me that you are truth and that truth is the only lasting authority. May my goals all be based on truth. I have found the principles of Jesus whom I call Lord to be truth. May I experience truth as it is revealed by love.

Amen!

August 31

Dear God,

Teach us through our experiences to be aware of reality. May we know and know we know that we may live by faith. May we be righteous in thought, word, and deed. Help us to truly repent of wrong thought, word, and deed. Since we know that all authority is in truth, may we always search for truth. May we turn away from all falsehood and turn to truth. Help us to learn truth and to do what we know to be right and to refuse or repent of what is wrong. May we believe in truth.

Amen!

# September

September 1

Dear God,

Help us to know right that we may live whole lives. May we seek to be whole in all areas of life. May we quit trying to impress others and start trying to be whole. May we come to realize that life is like a mirror. We get out of life what we put in. Help us to have integrity and to show it by treating all human beings whom we mingle with as we wish to be treated. May we not be ashamed of our reflection.

Amen!

September 2

Dear God,

Since you are the personification of truth, we want to know you. May we have truth as Jesus reveals truth. Help us to know truth that we may be transformed. May we overcome our ignorance that we may have integrity by avoiding mistakes. Give us the will to do good. Help us to be enlightened, that we may repent of wrong and turn to what is right. Give us knowledge, understanding, and wisdom and save us from ignorance, superstition, and falsehood. May we live more abundantly.

Amen!

September 3

Dear God,

Help me to think, speak, and act wisely. Help me to seek truth and to know when I have found it. May I inspire others to seek truth. Help me to grow in grace. May I not be ashamed to witness for the revelation of truth. Help me to do right and rejoice with a clear conscience. May I have the joy of living without guilt or disease. May I have the self-discipline to live more abundantly. Help me to know truth and make right choices.

Amen!

September 4

Dear God,

May we be given to truth as were the early followers of Jesus. Help us to live daily as though we were in the presence of Jesus. May we be guided by the Holy Spirit of truth and good will. May we be learners who inspire others to learn. May we make learners who obey your unchangeable laws, which control all life. Help us to avoid disease and frustrations that we may have unspeakable joy. Help us to have peace and hope. May we experience love and live by faith.

Amen!

September 5

Dear God,

Teach us to watch with open minds. May we see what is real and not some mirage. May we see with our minds and come to know that we know.

Help us to discern truth and to impart truth. May we be not deceived. May we never deceive intentionally. Help us to repent of error as soon as we learn we have erred. Teach us to know how to do good and to will to do good. May we not be as the priest and Levite, but like a good Samaritan. May we love others.

Amen!

September 6

Dear God,

May we become more like Jesus than like the Pharisees. May good deeds and attention flow from us. May we get to the place in life when we can give attention to others and not seek attention from others. May we not be out to exploit others, but out to help others. May we not worship idols by always seeking something, but help us to worship you by giving something. May we not lose our lives by trying to gain the world, but redeem the time by giving to others of our knowledge and our service.

Amen!

September 7

Dear God,

Help us to receive the life that comes from being born of God. May we receive knowledge, understanding, and wisdom and may we share with others what we have received. May we never share ignorance, superstition, falsehood, and ill will. May we help others and refrain from doing harm to anyone. Enlighten us that we may share what is good. May we live abundantly and share abundance with others. May knowledge, understanding, and wisdom flow to and from us. May we know you our God.

Amen!

September 8

Dear God,

You have given us minds to think with and bodies to work with. If we think through what life is and what truth is, we will know what to do and how to do it. Help us to be obedient in doing what we know to do and in not doing what we know is wrong to do. May we be sincere in following the path of good will. May we do good and not evil as long as we live. Help us to remember that we each have one life to live, and that we reap what we sow.

Amen!

September 9

Dear God,

Since you are truth and love, to know you is to seek truth and show love, which is good will toward others. Help each of us to follow Jesus in revealing truth and love to all with whom we do business. May we be sincere in all our dealings. May we never deceive or unjustly exploit another human being. We have learned that your laws apply to each of us. Help us to see all others as equals. May we not bow to others, nor depress others. May we each do the best we can, with what we have, where we are, so as to reveal truth and love.

Amen!

September 10

Dear God,

Help us to know that we know, so as to act on what we know. Be unto us a guiding Spirit of truth and love. May we live in obedience to truth and good will, and may we, by being good examples, teach others to obey your laws. May we not just talk of the Highway of Holiness, but also travel the Highway. May we not say one thing and do another. May we know we cannot hide from ourselves. Thank you for your revelation through Jesus and his followers.

Amen!

September 11

Dear God,

Help us to humble ourselves and allow the teaching of Jesus to enlighten our path. May we allow Jesus to be our example as we seek to live more abundant lives. May we each seek to live rich lives. May we each try to become a better example. May we not play games, but reveal the blessings that come by the faith, which is knowing we know. May we overcome our doubts and fears by seeking truth and showing good will.

Amen!

September 12

Dear God,

Help us to know truth. May we ask for what is helpful to all concerned. May we not seek special treatment but promote equality and justice. Help us to avoid all extremes. May we each be willing to see from the others' point of view. May we each be called your child because we are instruments of your peace. Help us each to go beyond the call of duty. May we each bear our own burdens and then have strength and will to help others.

Amen!

September 13

Dear God,

May I make good use of my time and means so as to finish my work. When I am judged, may I not be found wanting. Help me as an individual to cooperate with others in doing your will. May we each seek truth and show good will. Deliver me from the proud and haughty. May I continue to learn truth and apply truth with good will. Help me to sow good seed on good ground, for I know I will reap what I sow. Guide me by your Holy Spirit of truth and good will.

Amen!

September 14

Dear God,

I believe that you are ultimate truth. You are truth from beginning. You are eternal truth which has no end. Help me to abide by your eternal laws which govern reality. May my future be grounded in truth. Help me to overcome all ignorance, superstition, and deception or falsehood, and ill will. In as much as I believe Jesus of Nazareth personifies truth, I sincerely desire to follow him. Guide me by your Holy Spirit of truth and good will. May I always seek more truth and try to be helpful to all with whom I associate.

Amen!

September 15

Dear God,

Since you are eternal truth, and you have given me the breath of life, I love you and seek to be your bondservant. As a believer in eternal truth, I am bonded to you. I know that you are sincere, and I know nothing can separate me from your love. I thank you for your truth and love, which Jesus of Nazareth reveals to us. We know that Jesus is our friend because we believe that he reveals you to us through giving up his life rather than submit to ill will and deception.

Amen!

September 16

Dear God,

My mind is open to knowledge, to understanding, and to wisdom. I desire to know, to know I know, and to act wisely. I desire to avoid costly mistakes, to repent when wrong, and to remain confident when right. Help me to make wise decisions based on truth. May I not deceive nor be deceived. May I never waste time and effort with utopian dreams. May I never seek to do the impossible. May I not be confused. May I not act arrogantly on ignorance, superstition or falsehood. May I seek truth with understanding and wisdom.

Amen!

September 17

Dear God,

Since all of us have drives and emotions, we are all tempted to yield to the lusts of the flesh, the lusts, of the eye, and the arrogance of pride. Help us to be humble enough to see truth and not to act on ignorance, lust, and emotion. Give us open minds and fill them with knowledge, understanding, and wisdom. May we be thoughtful learners, and careful teachers of truth. May we repent of all wrong by turning from evil to good–from deception to truth.

Amen!

September 18

Dear God,

Thank you for Jesus. He is an adequate, and sufficient example. I want no better friend. I believe in him as one who reveals truth and opposes falsehood. Help me to follow him. I believe that you are the truth revealed through Jesus the Christ. May I continue to learn and to make learners. May your Holy Spirit of truth and love be my guide. May I seek you, honor you, bless you, praise you, and attribute worth to you.

Amen!

September 19

Dear God,

May the Lord Jesus, the revealer of truth and love, be my
constant companion. May I never turn aside from truth and love.
Help me to resist the temptation to be false or show ill will. Help
me to gain skill at proving what is good and to be faithful at doing
and inspiring good. Help me to be aware that I reap what I sow. May
I sow good seed on good ground that I may reap good. Help me to
be a good steward as I share good with others to meet their needs.
Amen!

September 20

Dear God,

Help me to be my best self. May I always remember who I see
in the mirror. May I be my friend. May I not blame others for my
mistakes. Help me to be mature and responsible. Show me how to
learn and teach. Show me what to do and how to do it. Show me
whom to serve and how to serve. Give me knowledge, understanding, and wisdom. Give me an open mind and good will. May
I have a good today and a better tomorrow.
Amen!

September 21

Dear God,

Thank you for being truth and good will. Thank you for the good
will of those who reveal you. Help me to reveal you to others. May
your truth and good will be seen in me. May my life and my smile
reflect your love. May my integrity reveal truth. May my humor
reveal truth. May I desire and reveal truth by all I think, say, and
do. May I make truth my authority. My God, and my Lord, be with
me as I pray.
Amen!

September 22

Dear God,

Help me to know who my Lord is. May I not be a hypocrite, but
obey the laws of God as revealed by Jesus and his church. Help me
to know truth concerning all I do and teach. May I not deceive or
be deceived. Help me do what needs to be done when it needs to

be done. May I and others continue to learn and to apply truth. May we become skilled and avoid error. Help us to repent when wrong and to excel when right.

Amen!

September 23

Dear God,

May we continue to advance toward what is believed to be Holy. May we seek wholeness whether in time or space. May we know the whole counsel of God. Help us to follow Jesus all the way.

May my life confirm truth as I seek to know and teach truth. When I have spoken may truth have been revealed. May my life until death reveal truth. May I be remembered as a true witness of the way, the truth and life.

Amen!

September 24

Dear God,

Help me to evaluate the work of my hands. May I cut off the activities that are not helpful to someone in some way.

Give me wisdom to work diligently and discretely. May I have integrity and be coordinated. Help me to gain skill and to persevere in doing what is right. May I do things decently and in order. Help me to be open-minded, congenial, and cooperative. May I enjoy life and enrich others. May I work toward health, wisdom, and prosperity for all my community.

Amen!

September 25

Dear God,

May I develop the wisdom that I need so as to cultivate friends. Help me to reach agreement with others lest they become enemies. Help me to learn diplomacy and to avoid conflict. Help me to know when to stand and when to run. May I do unto others as I expect others to do unto me. May I go a second mile to attain or retain peace. Help me to avoid or prevent anger and conflict. Give me the grace to turn the other cheek. Help me to relate properly to others. Give me humility and wisdom to learn and teach.

Amen!

September 26

Dear God,

Help me to live in harmony with those who seek to do good. May I always be ready to forgive those who repent of evil. Give me an attitude of gratitude. May I look for the good in people. Help me to learn truth, think truth, speak truth, and teach truth. May I be freed from all willful ignorance, superstition, folly, and ill will. Help me to learn truth and to know that I have learned truth. Give me wisdom and help me to gain skill. May I live a useful life. May I have good will, faith, and hope.

Amen!

September 27

Dear God,

I believe you are the essence of truth and that to know you is life. I accept truth as the ultimate authority. It is by knowing you that I can live an abundant life. Help me to experience you. Help me to avoid being controlled by deception, or ignorance, or superstition, or ill will. May I be guided by your Holy Spirit of truth and good will. May I give good, cheerfully and liberally. May I overcome all selfishness and greed. Help me to turn from all deception to truth. I choose to follow Jesus.

Amen!

September 28

Dear God,

To follow Jesus is my desire and my intent. Give me the knowledge, understanding, and wisdom that I need as I follow. May I seek until I find the way of truth and light. May I know I am on the right road, going in the right direction. May I have the will and patience to endure hardship, to face adversity, and to do what needs to be done to finish my course and keep the faith. May I follow Jesus as long as I live. May I walk in the comfort of the Holy Spirit.

Amen!

September 29

Dear God,

Thank you for the knowledge of the Apostle Paul. I, too, have a desire to preach the Gospel of the grace of God. As did Paul, I believe that your grace is sufficient to meet all our needs. May I always believe in your provision. What is needed you supply. Give us faith to accept your provision and the wisdom to promote your purpose. May we seek to prove what is good and to build our character by doing what is good. May we have faith, hope, and love.

Amen!

September 30

Dear God,

Guide us by your Holy Spirit of truth and good will. May we always love as Jesus loves. May we not forget to do unto others as we would have others do unto us, if our roles were exchanged. May we never seek an unfair advantage. May we know and remember that all things are under your control. May we know and obey your laws. May we so live as to make this a good day and tomorrow a better day. May we continue to live by faith and to grow in grace.

Amen!

# October

October 1

Dear God,

Thank you for the teaching and example of Jesus. By our following Jesus, we are able to enjoy the higher life. We thank you for the blessings we receive when we do as Jesus leads us to do. Help us to continue gaining knowledge, understanding, and wisdom regarding reality. May we be sincere, honest, and courageous as we live on more mature plateaus. May we grow in grace, faith, peace, love, wisdom, and hope. Help us to live abundantly.

Amen!

October 2

Dear God,

When our needs are many and our faith is small, we seek your mercy and your good will. Help us to carry our own burdens and to share the burdens of others. May we have attained the place in life where others' needs are able to elicit our mercy and compassion. May we cease to be arrogant and self-righteous. Thank you for your grace and truth. May we so live as to share your compassion and fellowship. May we be willing to suffer for what is right. Amen!

October 3

Dear God,

Help us persevere in doing right toward all people. May we persevere to the extent that we forget about personal comforts and pleasures as we seek to alleviate human suffering. May we recognize the urgency of our help. Help us to enjoy being of help to those in need. May we be as anxious to help as a thirsty animal is to find water. Help us share your provision in a healing manner. Thank you for your grace. Increase our faith. Amen!

October 4

Dear God,

Thank you for lifting us above the cesspools of life. May we use our time and resources in being good stewards of your grace. May we lift our eyes toward the higher things of life. May we become less and less sinful and more and more saintly. May we become so aware of your grace that we identify with you. Help us to repent more readily and to err less often. Thank you for calling us to be saints and helping us to live more abundantly. Amen!

October 5

Dear God,

I confess my sins and seek forgiveness. I confess that I have done at times what I should not have done, and I have left undone what I should have done. I have failed to mature in grace and truth. I have lacked faith. Give me more knowledge, more understanding, and more wisdom. Help me to have more faith and to grow in grace. May I be humble enough to learn what I should learn. May I be willing to do what I should do. Help me to love others and to do unto others, as I would have others do. Help me to be grateful. Amen!

October 6

Dear God,

Thank you for a good mind and a healthy body. Thank you for a good environment where there is an abundance of love and beauty. Thank you for a sense of law and order. Thank you for friends to share with and opportunities to help make improvements. Thank you for life, liberty, and the hope of happiness. May the world be richer each day as long as I live. Help me to accept and appreciate my lot in life. May I contribute to peace and prosperity. Help me to share cheerfully what I have.

Amen!

October 7

Dear God,

Help us to know him whom to know is life. Show us the way to overcome our sins. Help us to know the one who was willing to die rather than lead us in the wrong direction. May we follow him and be willing to die rather than lead someone astray. May we so live as to reflect the light of Jesus. May others see Jesus in us. May we be able to say with Paul, I know him in whom I believe. I seek to become more and more like him.

Amen!

October 8

Dear God,

When we fear we are losing our way, may we hear Jesus saying, come unto me. May we follow him and seek his guidance. May we know him as the way, the truth, and the life. May we be united with God and do his will. Help us to live enlightened and useful lives. May each of us control our passions and drives. May we follow Jesus in doing God's will. May our words and deeds reveal God's love, mercy, and goodness. May we be Holy, just, and true.

Amen!

October 9

Dear God,

May we seek truth and seek to teach truth by word and deed. May we be acceptable to you. Help us to accept your grace and live by faith. May we be your children and grow in grace as we live by faith. Help us to know and to know that we know that we may have more faith. Give us wisdom to live more abundantly. Help us to learn and to inspire others to learn. Help us to discipline ourselves to walk in the light. May we not stumble. Amen!

October 10

Dear God,

Thank you for revealing truth to the humble. May we not be conceited, but always humble enough to learn. May we never think of ourselves as being greater or wiser than others. May we learn and understand and grow wise. Help us to be kind, generous, and merciful. Help us to be grateful for all our gifts and to take advantage of our opportunities for growth in grace and truth. Forgive our sins and help us to forgive any who sin against us. May we love all our neighbors and do unto all others as we would have all others do unto us.

Amen!

October 11

Dear God,

Thank you for the healing service of Jesus. May we trust him as the way to be healed. Thank you for his wisdom. Thank you for giving him power to restore life and to help relieve anxiety. May we, like Jesus, learn to meet human need and to give hope to those in distress. Give us power and zeal to do your work and also patience to await your blessings. May we learn how and when to do what needs to be done. May we not hinder your work. Forgive our sins.

Amen!

October 12

Dear God,

May we, like Enoch, live in harmony with your laws. May we know that we are in harmony with truth. Give us more knowledge, more understanding, and greater wisdom. May we resist temptation to follow the crowds. May we walk with you. May we experience your love and mercy. May we have faith to believe in your provision. May we believe, as did Paul, that your grace is sufficient. Open our eyes that we may see. Open our ears that we may hear. Give us understanding and wisdom. Help us to live more abundantly.

Amen!

October 13

Dear God,

Help us to be aware of our responsibility to help others carry their burdens. May we appreciate those, like Moses, who give their lives helping slaves to become free. Thank you for those through the ages who have been good examples. May we admire and imitate worthy examples. Thank you for peacemakers who have been called your children. May we use our minds and means to help others to live more abundantly. Forgive us when we are too weak to resist the lusts of the flesh. Help us to walk by faith.

Amen!

October 14

Dear God,

May we obey the command of Jesus and make learners. May we learn ourselves and by example teach your truth so that by doing what is needed we may all live more abundantly. Help us to overcome ignorance, superstition, falsehood, and ill will, that we may be blessed. Help us to realize truth and overcome futility, falsehood, and failure. May we grow in grace and live by faith. May we believe in the authority of truth and obey your laws. Deliver us from evil.

Amen!

October 15

Dear God,

Help us to believe in the example and teaching of Jesus. May we learn the truth that sets us free to do right. Give us more faith. May we learn to accept what cannot be changed and to improve what can be changed. Help us to be good stewards of all you provide. May we each use truth to bless all concerned. May we enrich all who know us and be enriched by others with whom we mingle. Help us to make your goodness known. Forgive our sins and help us to be more grateful.

Amen!

October 16

Dear God,

Help us to utilize what you provide. May we not waste what is provided. Help us to work while it is day and to walk in your light. May we reap what has been sown. Give us what we need and guide us in what we do. May we bless and be a blessing to others. Be our Lord and help us to serve. May the thoughts of our minds, the words of our mouths, and the works of our hands be acceptable to you. Show us your love; teach us your truth; lead us to repent of our sins and forgive us and guide us.

Amen!

October 17

Dear God,

Help us to do the best that we can with what we have. May what we do reflect the light of Christ. May we be free from falsehood, and filled with the Spirit of truth and love. Give us knowledge, understanding, and wisdom to follow Jesus. May we advance his work. Help us to be true to our calling and to live by faith in Christ. May we be quick to hear, but slow to speak. Help us to be sincere and cheerful. May we persevere until we finish our course. Forgive our sins.

Amen!

October 18

Dear God,

May we, like the early disciples, do what we do in the character of Jesus. May we bear witness that we have faith in Jesus as we continue to seek truth. May we be among the righteous who live by faith and are called the children of God. May we promote peace and prosperity. Help us to love your people. May we love our neighbors as ourselves. May we seek to do unto others as we would have them do unto us. Help us to live righteous and Holy lives. Forgive our sins and help us to be grateful. May we be good stewards.

Amen!

October 19

Dear God,

Deliver us from the evils of this age. May we seek your kingdom, and do your will. Save us from our emotions and drives and from the lusts of the eye and the flesh. May we use our minds. Help us to practice self-discipline and self-control. May we prove what is good and refrain from seeking to be popular. May we not follow the crowd, but lead others to do right. May we have patience, and courage to persevere in doing right. Increase our faith.

Amen!

October 20

Dear God,

Help us to separate ourselves from falsehood. May we be able to discern truth. Help us to choose what is best and to do what is best. Give us more knowledge of truth, more understanding of truth, and more wise to apply truth. May we live in harmony with truth. Help us to use our time and our means to promote truth. May we be good stewards. Forgive our sins and help us to be grateful. May we know and know that we know.

Amen!

October 21

Dear God,

Give us more faith that we may accept your provision. May we see the results of your power. Help us to respond positively to all the truth we affirm. Help us to grow in grace. May we be grateful for all that is provided. May we use our skills and means to bring about what is good. Teach us to be wise. Help us to see our place of service and give us the means and motivation to serve. Help each of us to practice self-discipline and to continue to learn and to teach.

Amen!

October 22

Dear God,

Help us to understand your will and your way. We thank you for the truth that you reveal to us. Help us to seek truth until we find it. May we be set free from falsehood. May we follow Jesus and accept him as Lord and Saviour. May we bow to truth as Jesus reveals himself as truth. Help us to overcome ignorance, superstition, and ill will. Help us to love our neighbors as ourselves. May our words and our deeds be sincere and helpful to all concerned.

Amen!

October 23

Dear God,

May we be renewed. Help us to show that we believe in Jesus. Help us to leave the futility and fear of failure behind and to walk by faith. May we press on toward the highest goals. May we accept all your truth and be able to make wise choices. May each new experience lead to more faith. Forgive our sins and enlighten our minds. Help us to control our emotions and drives and to escape the destructive works of the flesh. Guide us by your Holy Spirit.

Amen!

October 24

Dear God,

We thank you that you gave us a way to verify truth, that we may know how to live abundant lives. We thank you for our perfect example, Jesus the Christ. Help us to know Jesus, to understand him, and to follow him. May we know the truth that sets us free from falsehood. May we accept the authority of truth and flee from idolatry. Give us knowledge, understanding, and wisdom to know truth and the will to obey. Help us to repent and to accept forgiveness. Amen!

October 25

Dear God,

Help us to be sincere with all that we may win some. May we not be discouraged when we seem to fail. Give us more proof of what is true, that we may have more faith. Help us to live by faith. May we never accept as true that which cannot be proved. May we be able to say with the Apostle Paul, "I know him in whom I have believed." To know Jesus as the way, the truth, and the life is the hope of salvation. Guide us by your Spirit of truth and love. Amen!

October 26

Dear God,

May we obey the command of Jesus as he obeys your commands. May we love as you love. May we will to do your will. May we choose to face reality that we may live wise, prosperous, and abundant lives. May we overcome doubt, futility, and fear. May our thoughts, words, and deeds be true to life. May we be not deceived nor deceivers. Give us direction, strength, and determination. May we persevere in truth and right relationships. May we bear the fruits of righteousness. Give us more faith. Amen!

October 27

Dear God,

May we learn truth and inspire truth. May we be followers of Jesus. May we live by faith. We believe that by your unmerited favor we have all that is needed. May we have faith to accept what you give us. Help us to use all things wisely. May we be good stewards. May we share cheerfully. Help us to help those who can and will use our help. May we be graceful and cheerful. Help us to be among the righteous who live by faith. Amen!

October 28

Dear God,

Help us to live in peace. May we be reconciled to any whom we may have displeased. May we help all our friends and neighbors to know and trust the prince of peace. May we enjoy good fellowship and be able to face reality. Forgive our sins and help us to forgive any who harm us. Show us how to live wholesome lives. May your Holy Spirit of truth and love be our guide and companion. Help us to continue to seek knowledge, to understand, and to apply wisdom.

Amen!

October 29

Dear God,

Thank you for Jesus. May each of us be grateful for all that he suffered for us. Thank you for letting us know that Jesus died to the flesh rather than lead us astray. May we follow him. We have hope of resisting temptation because Jesus set the example. Give us faith to resist temptation. May we ever be mindful of our Lord. Help us to keep his commandments. May we face suffering with patience and be grateful for strength to endure. When we face enemies, give us more faith.

Amen!

October 30

Dear God,

Give us faith that pleases you. May we be what you would have us to be. May we seek to live each day by faith. Help us to know and to know we know. May we understand and apply wisdom. Help us to shun evil and to overcome ignorance, superstition, falsehood, and ill will. May we be helpful to one another. Deliver us from fear, futility, and foolishness. May we have a good sense of humor and enjoy rich fellowship. Guide us by your Holy Spirit.

Amen!

October 31

Dear God,

Thank you for revealing yourself to me as the reality, which is the final authority. Help me to know you for what you are. Help me to know truth and to avoid all deception. May I continue to learn who and what you are and how I may relate to you. Help me to hear, to read, and to understand. Give me the will to do what you will for me to do. Help me to overcome when I am tempted to do wrong or neglect to do right. May I be guided by your Spirit of truth and love.

Amen!

# November

November 1

Dear God,

I realize that I am here as an object of your love and mercy. Thank you for your redemptive love and tender mercy. Thank you for sending Jesus to reveal your love. Thank you for giving us a perfect example to follow. Help us to follow Jesus and be examples for others to follow. May we repent of all known wrong. May we overcome ignorance, superstition, falsehood, greed, and ill will. Help us to relate properly to others by doing what is right toward all people.

Amen!

November 2

Dear God,

I love you and I show it by keeping your commandments. I pray for knowledge, understanding, wisdom and above all good will. May I control my emotions and drives and flee from lusts of the flesh. Help me to know what to do and give me good will to do it. Forgive me when I repent of mistakes. Help me to understand others and to live in peace as we share our lives with our neighbors. May I follow Jesus and teach others by being a good example. Guide me by your Spirit of love and truth.

Amen!

November 3

Dear God,

Help me to put to death my selfish desires and to cultivate the virtues that enrich life. May the way of Jesus be made known to and by me. Help me to know truth and to teach truth. May I show by example that I have been with Jesus the Christ. Guide me by your Holy Spirit that I may be your servant. Help me to die to what is wrong and to live for what is right. Help me to promote wealth and shun harm. May I be useful to you.

Amen!

November 4

Dear God,

Forgive me for not responding to your love. Help me to know and to do good. May I draw closer to you and feel the nearness of your presence. Help me to see and appreciate your good works. Give me a discerning mind and a responding good will. Help me to know your love and to reveal it to others. Help me to know more of your truth and to resist deception. May I learn to rightly divide truth. May I apply truth that is relevant. Help me to reveal your will.

Amen!

November 5

Dear God,

Help me today and every day to suffer for doing right. May all my suffering remind others that I am following Jesus. May I never suffer for doing wrong or not doing right. Help me to know and to understand your will and your way. Help me to show evidence to others that I trust you and that I appreciate your kindness and mercy. Help me to have patience when wronged and to persevere in doing right. May I never blame others for my sins.

Amen!

November 6

Dear God,

Help me to believe what I know to be true. Help me to resist all that I know to be false. Give me an inquiring mind and a keen sense of discernment.

Help me to show your grace when I rebuke wrong. Help me to have courage to openly oppose sin. May I persevere in right judgement and be not deceived. Help me to follow Jesus as he reveals the way, the truth, and the life. May each day reveal truth. Help me to remember that each day is a day for salvation. Help me to live in my day.

Amen!


November 7

Dear God,

Thank you for life, liberty, and a way of happiness. Thank you for being faithful in keeping your covenant. Help me to be faithful. Help me to live so as to show my love for you. May I be faithful in living so as to accept your grace. May I know, understand, and accept your will and your way. Help me to live by your truth and love. May your Spirit of truth and love guide me every day of my life. Help me to follow Jesus as he reveals your grace, mercy, and love.

Amen!


November 8

Dear God,

Help us to rejoice and be thankful for this day. May we do your will as we follow the guidance of your Holy Spirit. May we do unto others as we would have them do unto us. May we discern what is good, right, and true. Help us to be good stewards of all that you have given to us. Help us to learn and to teach. May we gain knowledge and understanding and be wiser. May we make few mistakes and do no deliberate wrongs. Forgive us and teach us we pray.

Amen!

November 9

Dear God,

May our sufferings remind us of the extent to which others have suffered for us. May we not suffer in vain. Thank you for giving us a perfect example in Jesus of Nazareth. May we learn more of him and follow his guidance. May we be true as he is true, and love as he loves. May we be willing to live for others and be willing to die rather than lead others astray. May we be willing to die for our friends. Help us to live righteously and uphold our convictions. May we be called peacemakers.

Amen!

November 10

Dear God,

Help us to become fellow workers in promoting equality. May we mature mentally until we see all humanity as one. May we reach a height in our thinking where we are one people in harmony with one God. May we come to realize to hurt anybody is to hurt everybody including ourselves. Help each of us to have part in building your kingdom. May all that we do bring glory to you. May we come to lose ourselves in doing your will. May we bless ourselves by blessings others. May we come to the place in life when with Jesus we live and die serving one another.

Amen!

November 11

Dear God,

Help each of us to go beyond primitive thinking. May we each reach a height in our plans where we will give ourselves for our children rather than expecting our children to give themselves for us. May we see beyond ourselves. Help each of us to grow in knowledge, understanding, and wisdom. May we see with Jesus the kingdom of righteousness. May we come to the vision of others as ourselves. Help us to experience what Jesus teaches. May we remember the truth of Jesus. May we sow what we want to reap.

Amen!

November 12

Dear God,

Thank you for renewing our spirits and giving us new hope. Thank you for Jesus, our example; help us to follow him.

Help us to see in Jesus the truth that sets us free from ignorance, superstition, falsehood, and ill will. May we know our mission and face reality. Give us knowledge, wisdom, and understanding. Help us to be good stewards and good ministers. Help us to do for our fellow beings what needs to be done to enrich their lives. Help us to repent of our sins and to accept your forgiveness. May we each have faith to accept your grace. May we learn to love every one. Amen!

November 13

Dear God,

Thank you for your Son who loved me and gave himself for me. May his love be shown in and through me. May I learn as he learned and grow as he grew. May I so live as to be his disciple. May I become a revealer of your truth and love. May I be guided by your Holy Spirit of truth and love. May I have fellowship with those who have been redeemed. Help me to attract good and to repel evil. May I be one of the peacemakers who are called your children. Amen!

November 14

Dear God,

May I be led by the Lord Jesus. May I walk in the light as he is in the light. May I come to know and understand truth and acquire wisdom to apply truth, as it is relevant. May I know when to say what needs to be said. May I know when to remain silent. Give me the wisdom and the courage that I need to do what I ought to do. Forgive my sins, and lead me in paths of righteousness. Help me to show gratitude by praising your name for all that you have done and are doing to enrich our lives. Amen!

November 15

Dear God,

Help me to live my own life and to allow others to live theirs. May I be a help and not a hindrance to true freedom for all. May I practice self-discipline and cooperation. Help me to make a contribution to society that will be beneficial to all. May I grow in grace and knowledge of truth. May I not deceive or be deceived. Help me to be a good steward of all you give me. Help me to be a good minister to those in need. Give me guidance and strength to do your will.
Amen!

November 16

Dear God,

Help me to always remember that I am a sinner saved by grace through faith. May I be forgiven and know that I am forgiven. Help me to be free from all guilt feelings. May I be free to do good under any and all circumstances. Give me a desire for the whole truth, and as you help me to always have good will, may all my thoughts, words, and deeds be free of prejudice and ill will. Thank you for your loving kindness and tender mercy.
Amen!

November 17

Dear God,

You have taught me that you are what you are, and that I am what I am. You are my Lord and master. I try to be your true son. I try to be realistic, as I believe a mature, sane, and sober person should be. I sincerely try not to deceive myself or others. I do what can be done and try not to waste resources. I try to work. Give me more vision, wisdom, and insight. Be with me. I trust you!
Amen!

November 18

Dear God,

Help me to know truth and to be free of all doubt. Help me to be real and to be free of all deception. Help me to be healthy and to be free of all disease. Help me to love honestly and to be free of ill will. Help me to think pure thoughts. Help me to speak kind words. Help me to act wisely. May I do what I know is helpful and shun what I know is harmful. Help me as I try sincerely to love others and to do unto others, as I would have others to do unto me. Forgive my sins and help me to be grateful

Amen!

November 19

Dear God,

May I face what is truth today. May I rejoice and be grateful. May I enjoy peace and tranquility throughout this day. May I gain knowledge of truth, understanding of truth, and wisdom to obey truth. Help me to be a channel for the blessings of truth. May I have the faith to accept and pass on your favors that I do not merit. Save me from the sins of willful ignorance, superstition, arrogance, and ill will.

In Jesus Name, Amen!

November 20

Dear God,

May I confess and repent of my sins that I may be forgiven. May all deception belong to the past. May I learn more truth. May I never be deceived by the lust of the flesh, the lust of the eye, or the pride of life. May I have good will and good health. May I be a good steward. May I have the guidance of your Holy Spirit as I seek to reveal truth and love. Thank you for your faithfulness. May I know, understand, and obey your laws.

In Jesus Character, Amen!

November 21

Dear God,

I have come to know you as the ultimate Truth, without beginning or ending—Always now. May I have fellowship with you and continue to be repelled by deception. May my thoughts, words, deeds, and attitude be in harmony with you. May I, like Jesus of Nazareth, and Paul of Tarsus, reveal you to others. May your will be my will. May I grow in grace, rejoice in truth and walk in love. May the road I travel be paved with your loving-kindness and the Guide for the journey be your Holy Spirit.

Amen!

November 22

Dear God,

May I so live as to make you known. May my life be a life of sharing with others for mutual benefit. May I overcome all self-centeredness and evil deeds. May I adhere to the teaching of Jesus. May I show good will to others as I would have them show love to me. May my neighbors and my family dwell in harmony with You. May we be the peacemakers that are called your children. Deliver us from the deception that would cause strife.

In His Name, Amen!

November 23

Dear God,

When we contrast and compare ourselves with all truth, we know you're worthy and we are contemptible. We confess our sins, repent of our sins, and accept your forgiveness. In as much as we are being saved, we know it is by our faith and a bestowal of your grace. We believe in you. We realize that we brought nothing into the age and we will take nothing out. Help us to be useful while we are here. May we grant to others all their due. Help us to love one another. Help me to be a doer of good and a channel of blessing.

Amen!

November 24

Dear God,

We believe that your grace is sufficient to supply all our needs. We pray that our faith may equal your grace so that our needs may be met. Give us faith to equal our needs. May we trust you. Help us to help others that all our needs may be met. May we have peace and prosperity. May we have fellowship as we live and work together. May we enjoy faith, hope, and charity. May we all seek ultimate truth and avoid all deception. Help us to live with an attitude of gratitude.

Amen!

November 25

Dear God,

Jesus, the Saviour, makes reality known. The purpose Jesus works toward is the revelation of truth or God. Jesus knows that, like the most enlightened of people living, he will continue learning until death. Jesus wills to learn. He teaches others to learn as long as they live. If we truly believe in Jesus, we dedicate ourselves to seek knowledge of truth, understanding of truth, and wisdom to apply truth as long as we are conscious. This is what I believe is praying in Jesus character.

Amen!

November 26

Dear God,

Thank you for Jesus, my Lord. I know Jesus is right. His principles satisfy my needs. It is by faith in truth as revealed by or through the life and work of Jesus that we are saved from fear and futility. Help me to seek truth and overcome falsehood or deceit as long as I am alive. I know that I cannot destroy truth. Help me to overcome ignorance, superstition, falsehood, and ill will that I may know truth or reality. I seek the whole truth as it is relevant to me. I trust reality. You are my God.

Amen!

November 27

Dear God,

Help me to put to death all falsehood or Idolatry. May I die to all that is false. Help me to stay alert to truth and receptive to your grace or provision of all that I need. May I share your grace by having faith in you. May I never be blind to truth or too greedy to share your blessings. Help me to overcome sloth and to help those who are weak or ill-informed. Help me to be united with all that is real or true and against all that is wrong.

Amen!

November 28

Dear God,

May I walk in my integrity. May I so live as to be an example of what is good, right, and true. May my words and deeds be consistent with reality. May I make it plain what is good for each person concerned. May I show brotherly love to my fellow human beings. May I face truth and shun deception in thought, word, and deed. May I habitually teach by life and work what is real, enriches life and shows wisdom. Thank you for your grace to give. May I give as I receive.

In Jesus Name, Amen!

November 29

Dear God,

To me, you are all that is good, right, and real. You are the existing truth. May my thoughts, words, and deeds portray you as you are to all who know me as I am. May others see me as a Godly person. May what I am remind others of what you are.

Thank you for being reliable. When I realize that your laws control all of life, I desire more knowledge, understanding, and wisdom concerning you. Give me more faith to know you.

Amen!

November 30

Dear God,

May I always be a good steward of your grace. May what comes from you be not wasted on lusts of the flesh and fun and pleasure. May I not live for the ego-self, but for the help of all humanity. Help me to see the needs of others and to have good will toward others. May I love my fellow human beings as myself. Help me to make Jesus Lord by doing unto others, as I would have them do unto me. May your blessings move to me and through me.

Amen!

# December

Dear God,

Help me to have integrity enough so as to obey all of your laws. May my life reflect your integrity. May I never practice hypocrisy. Help me to live so as to give evidence of facing reality. Since Jesus reveals you as reality by his doing your will, may people take note that I believe in Jesus. Help me to reveal truth by thought, word, and deed. May I seek truth, know truth, and reveal truth.

In Jesus Name, Amen!

Dear God,

Thank you for your unlimited reign. Thank you for the eternal, ever-present hope of better things to look forward to. I realize that at any time my relation to you is like a drop of water in the ocean. You have shown me that I am one among billions. I desire to be united with others so together we can be your church. I realize that I am but one cell in your body. I also realize that as a cell in your body, I will be replaced. Help me to be a good cell. May I be of service to other cells as I abide in you.

Amen!

Dear God,

May my words written or spoken be more than empty vessels that rub or bang. May they carry a message of truth. May my thoughts, words and deeds reveal truth or reality. Deliver me from falsehood. May I neither deceive nor be deceived. May I never manipulate others nor allow others to manipulate me. May I never coerce nor be coerced. Help me to maintain my integrity and good will. May I so live as to inspire others. May I, by word and deed, reveal my integrity. May I repent when wrong and stand firm when right.

In Jesus name, Amen!

December 4

Dear God,

Thank you for supplying all that we need. Help us to so live as to share with others as if we were all one. May we never think we are special.

Thank you, our God, for being impartial. May we each have self-respect and self-confidence. May we seek to live in obedience to all your laws so as to make life abundant for all. Help us to care for our needy people. May we be willing to share as equals. Help us to have good fellowship.

Amen!

December 5

Dear God,

Thank you for making it possible for each of us to be great in some way. May we do the best that we can, with what we have, where we are so as to be in harmony with you. May we be great in our giving and in our serving. May we practice the humility that leads to greatness. Forgive us for sometimes being too proud to receive. May we be exalted by humility and not be humiliated by false pride. May we humble ourselves and learn truth. May we come to know you better.

Amen!

December 6

Dear God,

Help us to know, understand, and wisely apply your laws that we may be in unity with you and do your will.

May we see your rainbow as the sun pierces the clouds. May we be reminded that Jesus is the light that we turn to in the midst of trouble, trials, stress, and distress. Help us to remember that you are faithful and that you do not change. May we follow the light of the world, Jesus the Christ, who reveals you to us. We trust Jesus, for we believe Jesus does your will. We pray in Jesus name.

Amen!

December 7

Dear God,

May our real sorrows lead us to repent of sin and enjoy good wholesome fellowship.

May we rise above strife and ill will and enjoy the bonds of peace. May we not be greedy but enjoy sharing our means with the needy that we all may be as equals. Help us to be good stewards. May we not indulge in evil pursuits, but think, speak, and act wisely.

May our sorrows lead us to repentance and restoration, lest we have loss and regret.

Amen!

December 8

Dear God,

May we, like Jesus, give our lives in obedience to your laws. May we have the vision and the knowledge, understanding, and wisdom to do your will. Help us to face life with faith, love, and hope. May we not be foolish and our efforts not be futile. May we overcome ignorance, superstition, and all that is false. May we have good will toward all our fellow beings. May we so live that your inner message may be, "Well done, good and faithful servant, enter into joy with your Lord."

Amen!

December 9

Dear God,

Bury our sins and resurrect us to a new life. May we walk in the spirit of truth and love. Help us to practice self-discipline and self-control. May we overcome our lusts and control our physical drives. May we never be controlled by the lusts of the flesh, the lust of the eyes, nor the pride of life. May we be humble to learn truth. May we obey your laws and do your will. May we lead others to you. May we never lead others astray. Help us to do what is good and right with what we have, where we are each day.

Amen!

December 10

Dear God,

Help us to know the truth that sets us free. May we never choose bondage to the evil of falsehood. Make us bond slaves to Jesus who is the way, the truth, and the life. May we bond with your laws and be separated from the deception of sin.

May we have insight and foresight. May we look outward, forward, and upward. Help us to gain knowledge, understanding, and wisdom that we may have faith in reality. May we be in harmony with all that is good, right, and true.
Amen!

December 11

Dear God,

Help us to see Jesus as our example. May we follow Jesus as he reveals you to us. May we not be deceived by our selfish inclinations. May we walk not after the flesh, but seek the guidance of your Spirit of wholeness. May we not mess up our lives trying to do the impossible or unreal. May we shun all that is false and seek all that is true. Help us to live wisely each day. May we not borrow trouble from the past or future. Give us peace in our time.
Amen!

December 12

Dear God,

Thank you for your integrity. I am grateful that you are all that is good, right, and true. I am thankful that you are pure and Holy, and that you and your principles do not change. Help me to know, understand, and be wise. May I be united with others who seek to do your will. May we work in unity and enjoy right relationships. May we love one another as you love us. May we stay united by bonds of peace. May we have faith in you and be saved from evil by your grace.
Amen!

December 13

Dear God,

May we pray without ceasing. May we be sincere in setting goals and persevere in trying to reach them. May we never set unreachable goals, though some goals may not be reached by us. May we have faith in you and realize that with you all things are possible. Knowing

our limitations, may we not think more highly of ourselves than we ought to think. Help us to remain humble that we may continue to learn; lest we become proud and lose our souls.
Amen!

December 14

Dear God,

May we, like Jesus, live peaceful lives. May we leave our peace with others so they will not be troubled by our having lived among them. It is my prayer that my lifestyle will promote peace. May I never cause trouble and strife. Should we find ourselves in warring camps, help us to negotiate peace. May we not value money, power, or honor more than human life. Help us to make peace and be called your children. May I never kill a fellow human being by intent or neglect. Help our nation to seek peace and cease building weapons of war.
Amen!

December 15

Dear God,

May I remain humble enough to study that I may discern truth and be wise. May I never become so arrogant as to assume truth without study. Help me to learn more and more as long as I live. Make me a learner and help me to teach others to learn. Bless all who learn to learn and would by example teach others. Help us to overcome ignorance, superstition, ill will, literalism, legalism, stupidity, and all other forms or types of deception. May we show evidence of having been with the Lord of truth. May ultimate truth be our only authority.
Amen!

December 16

Dear God,

May we, as taught by the Apostle Paul, arm ourselves for peace. May we value faith, truth, righteousness, and whatever else would make us Godly. May we stand against all that is evil and for all that is helpful. May we overcome all deceit and learn truth that each one of us may live more abundantly. Help us to know truth and to obey truth. May we use our minds and resist the lusts of the flesh. May we live prayerful or sincere lives. Deliver us from arrogance and foolishness. Give us a good sense of humor.
Amen!

December 17

Dear God,

Help us to grow as Jesus grew. May we learn and help others to learn. Help us to grow toward maturity. May we seek to live by God's eternal principles. May our thoughts, words, and deeds be realistic. May we have faith in you and be not deceived. As Jesus advised Peter, may we put Satan, or deception, behind us. May we be obedient to God's principles that we may bear good fruit. May we believe as Jesus and other Prophets taught that obedience is better than sacrifice. Help us to obey.

Amen!

December 18

Dear God,

We believe that, as your prophets have taught, all things work together for good to those who love truth. Help us to see you as the truth and love that we believe you are. Reveal yourself to us that we may overcome any doubt that we may have about your goodness. We believe that, since we are created from our planet Earth and are composed of the same elements as the earth, we live best when in harmony with our environment. Help us to experience reality without deception. Forgive our sins and guide us by your Spirit of truth and love. Heal us and inspire us we pray.

Amen!

December 19

Dear God,

It troubles me to read that Jesus once said, "I came not to send peace, but a sword." I hope he meant that he came not to send away peace, but a sword. Send usually mends to send away. Any way you interpret Jesus, you know that he stood for and not against peace. We are taught that the Sword of the Lord is truth. We win by promoting peace. The truth is the first victim of war. People at war deceive one another. Thus war is evil for it is against truth. Falsehood and Satan are one.

Amen!

December 20

Dear God,

Thank you for Jesus of Nazareth who taught us to look unto you for all that is good, right, and true. May we trust Jesus whom we believe knows the way, the truth, and the Life. We believe that Jesus shows us the only true reality. We believe that you, our God, are the reality. We believe that you are ultimate truth and the final authority. We believe that to know you is life, and to be separated from you is death. Help us to know you and live.

Amen!

December 21

Dear God,

Thank you for guiding us by your Holy Spirit of truth and love. May we follow your Spirit and enjoy your many blessings. May we be united with you and live in harmony with your laws. May we seek and find and do your will. May we be your children and citizens of your Kingdom. May we repent of all known sin and experience your complete forgiveness. May we be faithful stewards of all we receive from your bountiful hand.

Amen!

December 22

Dear God,

May we be drawn into union with Jesus. May we be as clay in your hands. Mold us into fit vessels for your service. May we be as open channels through which your blessings are carried. May we be part of your life and work. Help us to know, understand, and share your truth. May we help Jesus to reveal you to our generation. Thank you for life that is good and everlasting. May we enjoy your blessings and pass them on to the next generation. Increase our faith and enrich our lives is our sincere desire.

Amen!

December 23

Dear God,

May we come to appreciate the faith of Jesus. May we, like Jesus, be willing to die physically to reveal saving grace and truth. Help us to give our lives in your service that others may live also.

Forgive us for being greedy. Help us to help the needy. May we know who is in need, what they need, and how we can meet the need. May we be able to shun the greedy and help the needy. May we help the rich to get poor as the rich help the poor to become rich. May we all become rich in knowledge understanding, and wisdom.

Amen!


December 24

Dear God,

May we magnify Christ and help him to magnify you. May we make your works visible and our egos invisible. Help us to choose to see rather than to be seen. May we not only have sight, but also have foresight and insight. Help us to be actors seeking results not play actors seeking attention. May we have a sense of humor and avoid foolishness. Help us to value life too much to waste it playing the fool. Give us more knowledge, understanding, and wisdom. Help us to overcome the foolish and the false.

Amen!


December 25

Dear God,

Thank you for all the young women who bear children who remind others of your presence. Thank you for Jesus, who always does your will, and reveals your presence. May many of us come to know Jesus and thus increase our faith. May we overcome any doubts about your love and mercy. Help us to accept the revelation of Jesus and live by faith in you as ultimate truth and final authority. Help us to sow good seeds. Help us to be mindful that we reap what we sow.

Amen!

December 26

Dear God,

Help us to walk with Jesus. May our thoughts, words, and deeds, be like those of Jesus. May we, like Jesus, walk in the light and avoid the works of darkness. May we not only gain knowledge, but also gain understanding, and wisdom. May we not only grow physically and mentally, but also grow socially and spiritually. May we be united with God the Father who creates, God the Son who redeems, and God the Spirit of truth and love who guides and comforts. May we overcome all sin and abide in truth.

Amen!

December 27

Dear God,

May we who have lost our way, like the Prodigal son, say, "I will return to my Father and plead for his mercy." May God forgive our sins and re-admit us into the household of faith.

May we, like Israel, return to the God of our Fathers. When we go astray, may we repent. May our sins be forgiven and our right minds be restored. May the Holy Spirit of Jesus return to our lives and lift us out of the doldrums and into the freshness of Spirit that we may move on.

Amen!

December 28

Dear God,

May we be converted and become innocent and humble. Like little children, may we be eager to learn and thankful for our growth. May we grow in every way. May we never become proud and haughty. May we be humble enough to learn whatever we need to know. May we be wise enough to forget what we need to forget. Help us to know what needs to be done. Help us to know how to do what we need to do. Help us to follow Jesus and to be guided by the Spirit of wholeness. May we help others to live richer lives.

Amen!

December 29

Dear God,

May we be willing to make a complete commitment to follow the Lord. May we never seek a shallow life when we can be immersed in the good will of Jesus. May we never evade truth nor seek falsehood. Give us the will to suffer in the flesh as we gain knowledge, understanding, and wisdom. May we, with Peter, realize that Jesus Christ has the words of life. Help us to seek the truth that sets us free from the bonds of sin. May we repent and accept your forgiveness. Help us to be grateful.

Amen!

December 30

Dear God,

May we drink deeply from springs of fresh living water. If life seems shallow may we dip a little deeper in the well. May we drink from fountains of pure water. May we wade deep into the waters of life flowing from your throne.

May we give of the water of life. May we share all that is good. May we help others to learn of your love. May we be learners and teachers. Help us to discipline ourselves and to teach by example. May we by faith experience your grace and pass it on.

Amen!

December 31

Dear God,

Thank you for being with us this year. We repent of our sins and ask for your forgiveness. May the New Year be used by us as the accepted time. Help us to have an attitude of gratitude. May we be good stewards of all we possess or acquire. May we show ourselves approved by rightly dividing words of truth. "May the words of our mouths and the thoughts of our minds be pleasing to you." Help us to do what we can, with what we have, where we are under the guidance of your Holy Spirit.

Amen!